The Kushite Cemetery of Sanam:
A Non-Royal Burial Ground of the Nubian Capital,
c. 800-600 BC

Angelika Lohwasser

This title is published by
Golden House Publications

© Angelika Lohwasser

All rights reserved

No part of this publication may be reproduced or transmitted in any form or by any means, digital, electronic or mechanical, including photocopy, recording, or any information storage and retrieval system, without permission in writing from the author.

English language editor: Paul Whelan

Frontpage: Udjat-composition (grave 0893, Museum Brussels 5714/4, photo: Lohwasser)
Backpage: Openworked plaque (grave 1188, Museum Brussels 5716/24, photo: Lohwasser)

Printed in the United Kingdom
by

CPI Antony Rowe
Bumper's Farm
Chippenham
Wiltshire SN14 6LH

London 2010

ISBN 978-1-906137-16-8

For

Martin

and

Anton, Flora and Emil

Contents

Colour figures:
Front page: Udjat-composition (grave 0893, Museum Brussels 5714/4, photo: Lohwasser)
Back page: Openworked plaque (grave 1188, Museum Brussels 5716/24, photo: Lohwasser)

1 Incense burner (Egyptian Museum Berlin, Inv. no. 7870, photo: Lohwasser)
2 Bead net (grave 0179, Ashmolean Museum no. 1921.846, photo: Grajetzki)
3 Decorated solid earring of faience (grave 1062, Ashmolean Museum no. 1921.627, photo: Grajetzki)
4 Sewing plaque (?) (grave 1095, Museum Brussels 5724/2, photo: Lohwasser)
5 Two more elaborated beads (Egyptian Museum Berlin, photo: Lohwasser)
6 Several tone beads (Egyptian Museum Berlin, photo: Lohwasser)
7 Barrel beads with painted decoration, (grave 1516, Ashmolean Museum Nr. 1920.196, photo: Grajetzki)
8 Various beads (modern strung, grave 0663, Museum Brussels 5710/12, photo: Lohwasser)
9 Various beads (modern strung, grave 0015A, Museum Brussels 5701/10, photo: Lohwasser)
10 Poppy pendants of carnelian (grave 0231, Egyptian Museum Berlin Inv.-no.3192, photo: Lohwasser
11 Fish-and-flower-pendant (grave 1062, Ashmolean Museum no. 1921.627, photo: Grajetzki)
12 Necklace with amulets and beads (grave 0337, modern strung, Museum no. 1921.513, photo: Grajetzki)
13 Udjats from faience and jaspis (graves 0714, 0120; Egyptian Museum Berlin 2922, 3119, photo: Lohwasser)
14 Udjat in openwork (grave 0722; Egyptian Museum Berlin 7823, photo: Lohwasser)
15 Quadruple-udjat (grave 1516 Ashmolean Museum no. 1914.475, photo: Grajetzki)
16 Amulet-plaques of Khonsu (grave 0722; Egyptian Museum Berlin 7815, photo: Lohwasser)
17 Frog (grave 1516, Ashmolean Museum no. 1914.478, photo: Grajetzki)
18 Decorated pot (grave 218, Ashmolean Museum no. 1921.478, photo: Grajetzki)
19 Napatan pot (grave 0143, Museum Brussels 5703/4, photo: Lohwasser)
20 Alabastron (grave 0337, Ashmolean Museum no. 1921.514, photo: Grajetzki)
21 Alabastron (grave 0337, Ashmolean Museum no. 1921.517, photo: Grajetzki)
22 Mirror (grave 0632, Ashmolean Museum no. 1921.623, photo: Grajetzki)
23 Jug from the Mediterranaean (grave 1416, Ashmolean Museum no. 1921.989, photo: Grajetzki)
24 Plaque (grave 1516, Ashmolean Museum no. 1914.465, photo: Grajetzki)
25 Plaque (grave 1516, Ashmolean Museum no. 1914.463, photo: Grajetzki)

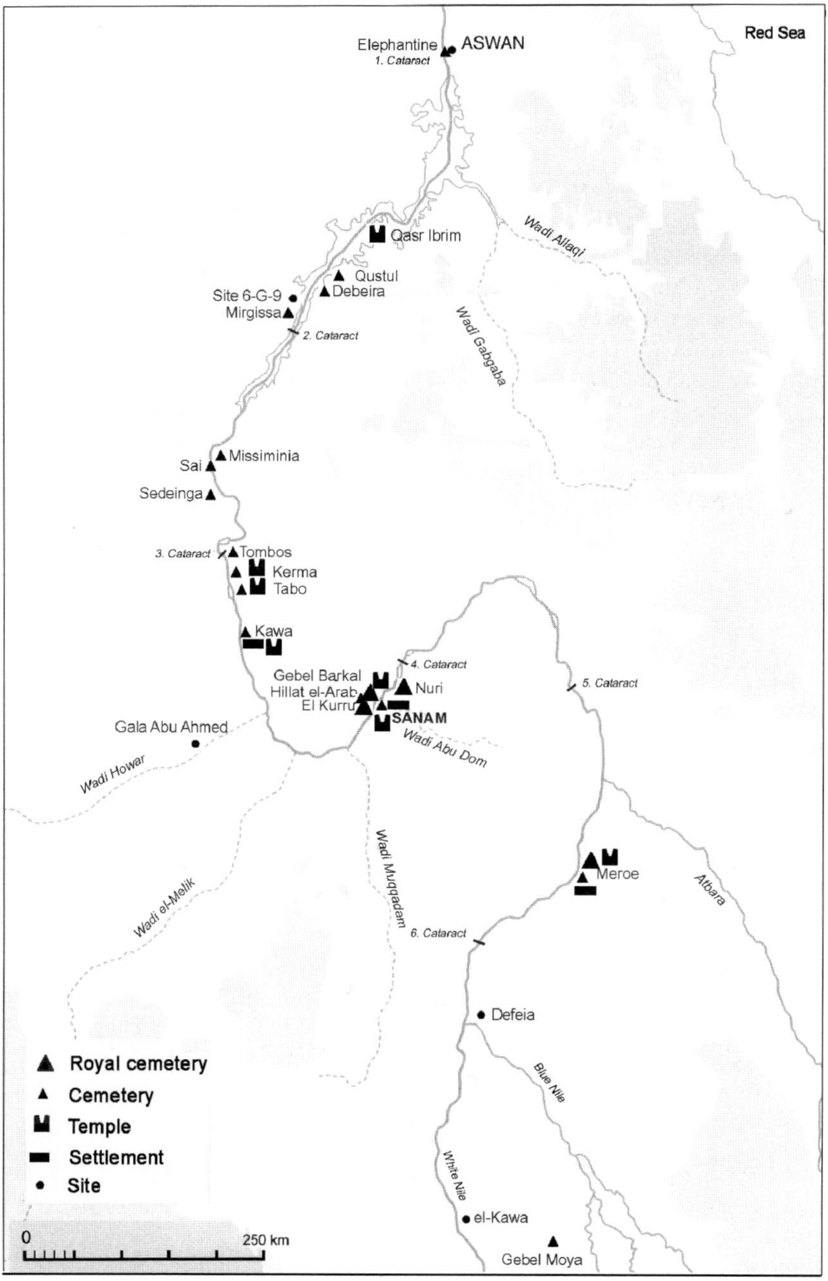

Map of Napatan sites (after maps in Sudan & Nubia)

Foreword

From 1998-2000 I had the chance to work at the Egyptian Museum Berlin and while there it was Karl-Heinz Priese who drew my attention to some finds from Sanam, stored in the magazine of the museum. My first research program, to collect and study all of the objects from Sanam, was soon postponed, since the overwhelming mass of the material as well as the difficulties in tracing parts across museums, private collections and the antiquity market made clear that it would last a long time and require extensive contacts. Nevertheless, I continued to work on the cemetery of Sanam, but with a narrower focus: analysis of the documentation of the excavator F. Ll. Griffith. His tomb cards as well as photographs and a plan of the cemetery are preserved in the Griffith-Institute, Oxford. The result of this study forms the subject of this volume.

I am especially grateful to Karl-Heinz Priese as well as to Dietrich Wildung, former director of the museum, for all their support and for permission to publish the photographs of objects here.

I made two research journeys to the Rijksmuseum van Oudheden, Leiden, and the Musées Royaux d'Art et d'Histoire, Bruxelles. I am greatly indebted to their curators, Dr Maarten Raven and Dr. Luc Limme. Moreover, I want to thank Helen Whitehouse for permission to publish photographs of the objects in the Ashmolean Museum and Wolfram Grajetzki who went there to take the photographs.

Twice I had the possibility to stay in the Griffith Institute in Oxford, and I want to thank Jaromir Malek as well as Alison Hobbes and Elizabeth Fleming for all their support and permission to publish some of the Griffith photographs here.

Many colleagues in Berlin and all over the world (international conferences help to communicate!) discussed specific subject areas with me. I cannot mention all of them, but *pars pro toto*: Dr. Petra Andrassy, Prof. Dr. Manfred Bietak, Dr. Julia Budka, Dr. Martin Fitzenreiter, Dr. Jana Helmbold-Doyé, Dr. Tim Kendall, Prof. Dr. Claudia Näser, Dr. Pam Rose, Prof. Dr. Helmut Satzinger, Dr. Anne Seiler, Dr. Stuart T. Smith, Dr. Irene Vincentelli, Prof. Dr. Steffen Wenig, Dr. Bruce Williams, Dr. Pawel Wolf.

For comparative analyses of the data I used the program WinBASP, written by Irwin Scollar (University Bonn). Prof. Dr. Stephan Seidlmayer introduced me to the program and the complex applications it could run. For this aspect of my study as well as for discussions and his acceptance as reviewer I owe him a special debt of gratitude.

A two-year-grant from the German Research Foundation allowed me to concentrate on this study, which I gratefully acknowledge, together with the grant towards the print costs.

Stephen Quirke and Paul Whelan kindly read the English version, Wolfram Grajetzki accepted the book for Golden House Publications.

The investigation of the cemetery of Sanam was presented to the Department of History and Cultural Studies of the Free University Berlin as Habilitation thesis. The full research publication will appear in German. This English version offers a comprehensive summary, representing all parts of the study, but with reduced discussions. Nevertheless, with this book I aim to provide a new introduction to a classic Kushite middle-class cemetery in all its complexity.

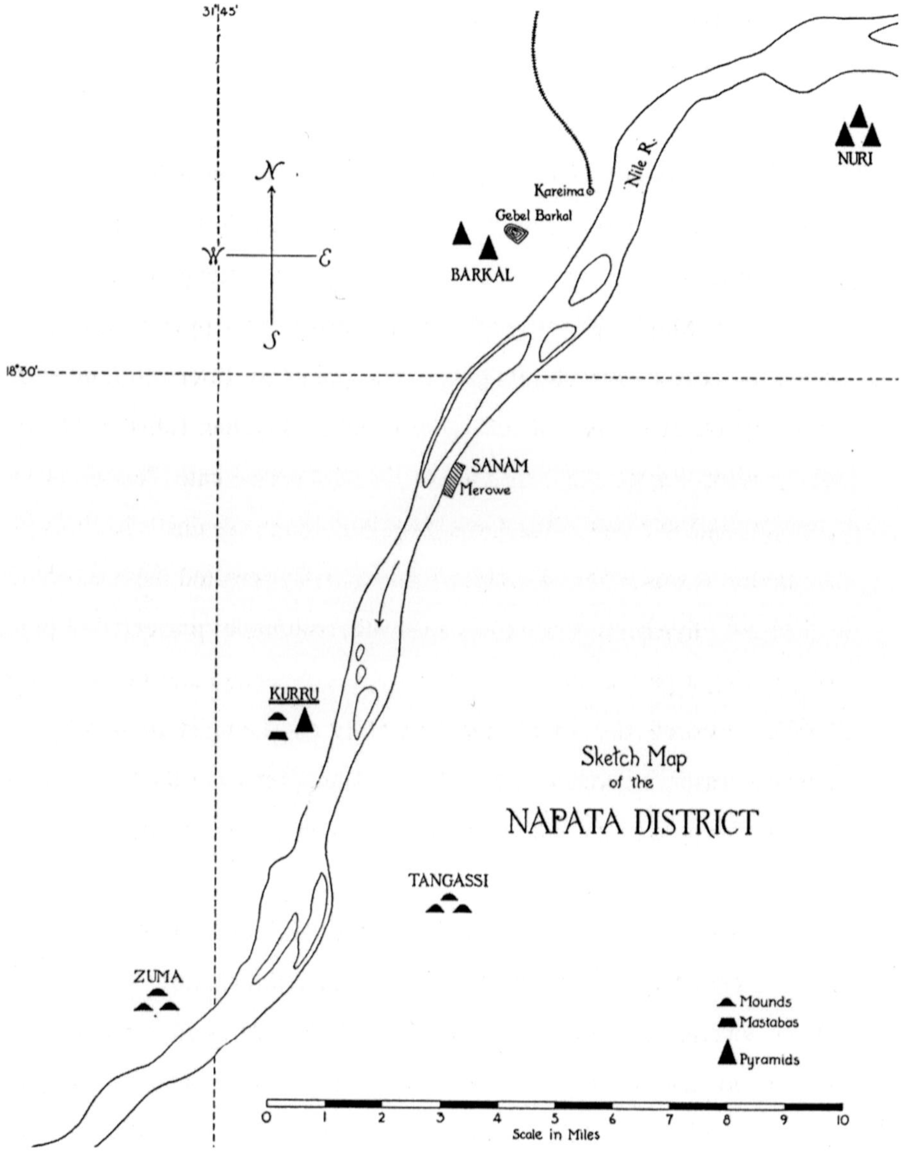

Fig. 1: Map of the region of Napata (after: Dunham 1950: Map I)

I. The cemetery of Sanam – the setting

I.1. Introduction

In the 9th Century BC a Kushite family came to power near Jebel Barkal in modern Sudan, and enlarged their sphere of control further to the north.[1] In the mid-8th Century BC they reached the Egyptian border at Elephantine. Maybe Kashta had already conquered Upper Egypt, but it was his successor Piye who fought battles against the rulers of Middle and Lower Egypt. In around 732 BC he defeated his last foe, Tefnakht of Sais, and reunited Egypt thus ending the Third Intermediate Period. When Tefnakht and his son Bocchoris revolted again against the Kushite domination it was Piye's successor Shabaqo who defeated them, and with it the 24th dynasty, and reinstated full pharaonic power in Egypt, inaugurating a period known as 25th Dynasty. Shabaqo and his successor Shebitqo restored monuments and reinstalled the administration in Egypt. Their successor Taharqo was able to build temples from the Delta in the north of Egypt to Upper Nubia in Sudan, although the second half of his reign was marked by the military campaigns of the Assyrian Empire directed against Syria, Palestine and Egypt itself. This Pharaoh left the old ancestral cemetery in El Kurru and built his pyramid in Nuri.

After several campaigns the Assyrians finally defeated Taharqo, who escaped to the south. His successor Tanwetamani again conquered Memphis and parts of the Delta, but was soon driven out of Egypt and back to the south. The Assyrians destroyed Thebes in 663 BC and installed Psammetich I as the new king.

We do not know the fate of Taharqo and Tanwetamani in Nubia, but their

---

[1] For the history of the Napatan Period in general see: Priese 1996, Török 1997, Kendall 1999, Morkot 2000, Lohwasser 2001, Zibelius-Chen 2006.

successors ruled there over an empire which stretched from the Butana in the south to Lower Nubia in the north. We know the names of most of the kings and queens, because their names were found on several items of their funerary equipment. However, except for Anlamani, Aspelta, Irikeamanote, Harsiotef and Nastasen, we know virtually nothing about their reigns. These five kings are better known to us because they left long inscriptions recording specific events. The kings following the 25th Dynasty in Nubia were buried in Nuri, the cemetery founded by Taharqo. In the 3rd Century BC the royal cemetery was transferred to Meroe, where the Meroitic kings and queens were buried until the 4th Century AD.

We recognise this break in the tradition by calling the earlier phase "Napatan" – when the burial ground is situated near the northern centre Napata – and the later phase "Meroitic", when the burial ground is near Meroe. However, we have to bear in mind that the capital, the administrative centre and the governmental seat of the kings, were located at Meroe at least since the reign of Aspelta, and perhaps even earlier.

I divide the Napatan Period into Early, Middle and Late. Early Napatan is pre-25th Dynasty and the 25th Dynasty up to Tanwetamani, which combine the phase of emergence of the kingdom – of which we know little – and the period of rule over Egypt, marked by the growing adoption of Egyptian elements and variations in the indigenous culture. The climax of this process is the reign of Taharqo. The two centuries following the retreat of the Kushites from Egypt, from Atlanersa to the reign of Irikeamanote, I call Middle-Napatan phase. The inscriptions are written in Late Middle Egyptian and in the depictions we can recognise the introduction of increasingly non-Egyptian traits. I propose calling the 150 years after Irikeamanote's reign up to the transfer of the royal cemetery to Meroe the Late-Napatan phase. The written language is a kind of regional dialect and in the material culture as well as in artistic depictions the Egyptian aspect is reduced even more.

List of selected kings (after Zibelius 2006: 496):

Kashta	*c*. 765-753 BC.
Piye/Piankhi	*c*. 753-722 BC.
Shabaqo	*c*. 722-707 BC.
Shebitqo	*c*. 707-690 BC.
Taharqo	690-664 BC.
Tanwetamani	664-*c*. 655 BC.
Atlanersa	2nd half 7th Century BC
Senkamanisken	
Anlamani	
Aspelta	1st half 6th Century BC
Aramatelqo	
Malonaqen	
:	
:	
Irikeamanote	2nd half 5th Century BC
Baskakeren	
Harsiotef	1st half 4th Century BC
:	
:	
Nastasen	335-*c*. 315 BC

I.2. The landscape (fig. 1)

The site of Sanam is situated about 25 km south of the the 4th cataract. The environment in the cataract region is harsh and barren. Rescue archaeology here brought to light a number of Palaeolithic, Neolithic and Kerma sites, all of small size. The Napatan and Meroitic Periods are even less well represented; only a few sites can be dated to these times. The bulk of the remains are of Christian and Islamic date.

South of the 4th cataract, the landscape is somewhat softer and more fertile, but the cultivated land is still only a small strip near the Nile. We do not know if the arable area was larger in antiquity, but many sites between the 4th cataract and Korti date to the Napatan and especially Meroitic Periods.

The river Nile, which starts in Central Africa and discharges into the Mediterranean Sea, flows directly south to north along most of its riverbed, but between Abu Hamed and Korti, the river changes its course and flows from north to south. Since in the Middle Nile Valley as well as in Egypt the south-north direction of the Nile constitutes the orientation of sacral buildings, the "wrong" direction in the area around the Jebel Barkal causes some confusion. This divergence between magnetic north and river north is reflected in the orientation of temples and their decoration at the Jebel Barkal, and may also have influenced the orientation of some of the tombs at Sanam.

The most important locality in the Jebel Barkal region is the "Holy Mountain". Many temples are situated around this 90m high mesa, dating from the New Kingdom (Thutmosis III, Ramses II), the Napatan Period (Early and first half of Middle Napatan) until the Meroitic Period (Natakamani and Amanitore). The most impressive buildings are temples, but there are also palaces situated in the sacral area. Beside the mountain two pyramid fields are arranged as well as some less visible funerary structures.

Located about 12km downstream of Jebel Barkal, the site of El Kurru contains the tombs of the kings and queens of the early Napatan period. The post-Meroitic tumuli of El Zuma are again some kilometres further downstream.

On the left bank of the Nile, 7km upstream of Jebel Barkal, in the large cemetery of Nuri, are buried the kings and queens of the Middle and Late Napatan Period. The cemetery was initiated by Taharqo, who built his tomb with the largest pyramid of the Middle Nile Valley there. The site of Sanam is situated about 12 km south of Nuri. Apart from the cemetery, a temple of Taharqo and a town with some administrative buildings have been found there. These structures will be discussed in detail in chapter II.1.3. Another 10 km downstream of Sanam the huge tumuli of Tangasi mark the burials of some Post-Meroitic rulers. Inland, 14 km east of Sanam, the Coptic cloister of Ghazali is situated in the Wadi Abu Dom. We can see that the region of Sanam was inhabited over a long span of time. Several monuments, temples as well as royal burials, form the sacral landscape.

I.3. The location (fig. 2)

Today, the cemetery of Sanam is buried beneath the modern town of Merawi. The necropolis lies very close to the Nile. The river could not have been far different in antiquity, since on the right bank there are elevations behind a narrow band of fertile land. Visible about 0.5 km north of the cemetery are the ruins of the temple, and again 0.5 km to the northeast the ancient town once stood. The measurements of the excavated part of the cemetery are 350 m x 150 m. The excavators recorded that the

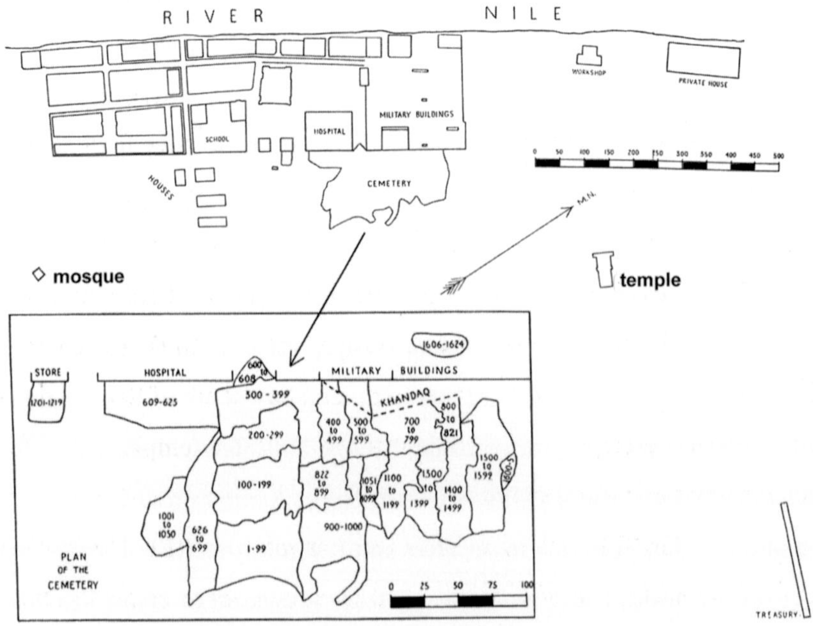

Fig. 2: Map of Sanam (after Griffith 1923: pl. XII)

area in the southwest is superior to the rest of the cemetery, but the precise difference is never mentioned. The soil is hardened sand, called *gebel* by Griffith, but never as hard as stone. It was possible to dig chamber graves and shaft tombs. The northern part of the cemetery is covered with loose sand. Most of the tombs here were never dug deep enough to reach the gebel.

I.4. History of research

In the time of the early 19th century travellers, a visit to the monuments at Jebel Barkal as well as those in the royal burial grounds in El Kurru and Nuri was a regular occurrence at least for those Europeans who ventured so far south. Several pioneers described or illustrated the ruins, but it was not until the Royal Prussian Expedition, led by Karl Richard Lepsius, that the site of Sanam was mentioned. Lepsius published a sketch of the ruins of the temple and a short description.[2] The cemetery was not seen by Lepsius, but it was mentioned by Bayard Taylor, an American journalist and traveller, who visited the site in 1852. He seems to have found a tomb, writing "The sand evidently conceals many interesting objects. I saw in one place, where it had fallen in, the entrance to a chamber, wholly below the surface."[3] Even after Lepsius, the site of Sanam was hardly prominent in the scientific literature. E. Wallis Budge, who, in 1897, stayed in the capital of the district of New-Merawi immediately south of Sanam, gave a very detailed description of the modern town and the temple, but did not mention any tomb or other ruin.

Francis Ll. Griffith arrived at Sanam in late autumn 1912. There was no sign on the surface to indicate the presence of a large cemetery, but in several lootings inhabitants of the town found by chance some graves and objects. Some of the finds, including bronze vessels and amulets, were presented to Griffith and he decided to excavate the cemetery and the visible temple of Sanam.

I.4.1. The excavation by F .Ll. Griffith

The third season of the "Oxford Excavation in Nubia" took place at Sanam after two seasons at the Lower Nubian site of Faras. The excavations of Griffith started in the cemetery on the 24th November 1912 and ended at the temple in March 1913. Griffith hoped to be able to continue his excavation, but the outbreak of the First World War prevented his return. After the war, the concession for the whole region was assigned to George Reisner, who excavated the temples at Jebel Barkal as well as

---

[2] LDT V: 282-286, LD V: 141.

[3] Taylor 1893: 434.

the royal tombs at El Kurru, Nuri and Barkal, but never undertook any work at Sanam.

Griffith excavated three areas at Sanam. He started with the large cemetery, and before these excavations ended he began to expose the temple. His last project was the clearing of parts of the so-called treasury, but he did not have time to finish this excavation.

The excavation of the cemetery took place between November 24th 1912 and February 1913. Griffith and his second wife Nora were the only European supervisors at the site, since the proposed assistant Leonard Woolley left for his excavations at Karkemish in Turkey. In nearly three months and with the help of some excellent *reis* (Egyptian heads of the workmen) from Quft and about 20 workers, they excavated around 1550 tombs. They were not able to clear the whole area of the cemetery, since small parts were buried under a hospital as well as under the main road.

I.4.2. The documentation

Today, the documentation of the excavation is stored in the Griffith-Institute, Oxford, and comprises:

–about 1600 pages with handwritten tomb cards with sketch-drawings

–the text of the tomb cards typewritten in a revised form and corrected by Griffith. In comparison with the handwritten tomb cards it is easy to see that Griffith checked every entry with photographs and sketches.

–216 cards with photographs and copies of sketches, where the inventory of certain tombs was recorded. These cover only a selection of the tombs and the finds

–plan of the cemetery, up to now unpublished

–about 600 photographs in an album, most of them already put on the 216 cards with photographs. Additionally, there are several photographs with details of bones made for Dr. Armand Ruffer, a physical anthropologist. The report of Ruffer is not stored at the Griffith Institute.

-an envelope with clippings of articles written about an exhibition put on after the excavation. The envelope also contains a list of benefactors with the distribution of objects to museums and antiquarians. The documents of the administration of the excavation (licence) is missing.

After the excavation, many of the objects were distributed to sponsoring institutions. Today finds from the cemetery of Sanam are stored in the following museums:

Ägyptisches Museum Berlin, National Museum Khartoum, Ashmolean Museum Oxford, Pitt-Rivers Museum Oxford, Fitzwilliam Museum Cambridge, Bolton Museum, Manchester Museum, Brighton Museum, British Museum London, Petrie Museum London, Staatliches Museum Ägyptischer Kunst Munich, Antikenmuseum Basel, Rijksmuseum van Oudheden, Leiden, and the Musées Royaux d'Art et d'Histoire, Brussels.
Some objects were given to private sponsors such as Freiherr von Bissing, Wilhelm Spiegelberg and Henry Wellcome. Today, these objects are difficult to trace. For example, the collection of von Bissing highlights the problems, since only a part of his collection was given to the Staatliches Museum Ägyptischer Kunst Munich. Another part was sold to the Egyptian collection in Leiden, while the scarabs were given to the Antikenmuseum Basel. Even now some of the objects of the former collection of von Bissing have still not been traced, for example not a single pot has been found.

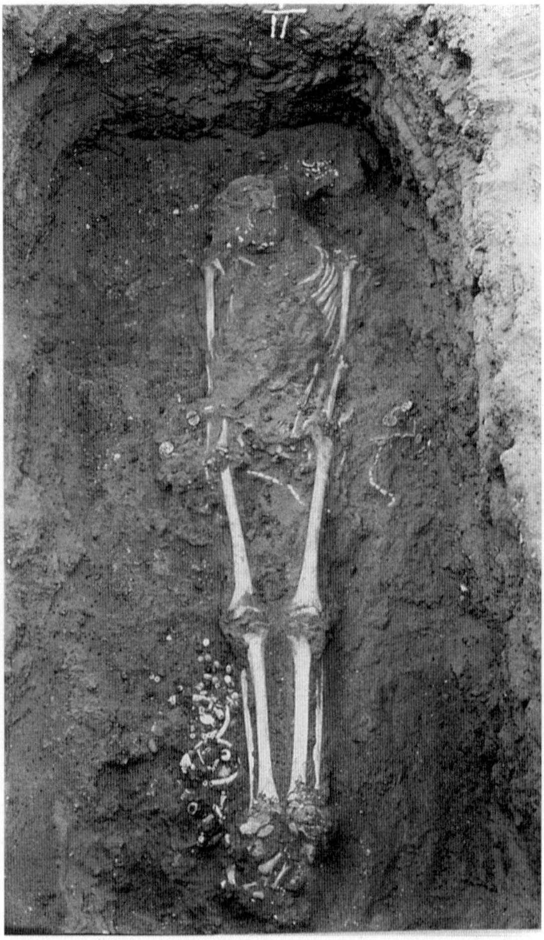

Fig. 3: Photograph of grave 0011 (left, photo: Griffith-Institute); entry in the tomb cards as well as the published entry of Griffith (1923: 142, below and next page) for grave 0011.

11. (Bln.) Rectangular grave in gebel with rounded corners, no trace of bricks, 174 by 71, D. 36. Axis 280. Young skeleton probably female, extended on back, hands on thighs head to river. L 113. Skull crushed.

Abundant ornaments, most of faded glass: - Above head, left of skull, (1) green glaze aegis of Isis; several uzat (one blue), one with black details, the others open work; flower and disc beads, the flower beads separated by red glaze ring beads; two globular beads of chalcedony, two of carnelian, shells of Engina mendicaria. Outside left hand (2), outside right hand (4) from right hand to chest (6), and beneath pelvis (7), a string of blue glaze disc beads, pierced quadruple uzats, and one imitation cowrie, original order preserved; with them, two cowrie shells (Cynraea annulus); and hatched cylinder bead.

Under right femur (4) shell of Mamilla melanostoma; glaze uzat, dwarfBy right hand (5), remains of glass(?) ring with oblong bezel (Anmerkung handschriftlich auf Kopie O unleserlich). On chest, (6) three ball beads of yellow paste, besides green glaze disc, flower beads, quadruple uzats etc. (see 2). Beneath pelvis, (7) see (2) Outside right tibia in a heap, (3) string of ostrich shell disc beads; green glaze hatched cylinder beads, two tubular beads; melon bead, right hand; sistrum; papyrus stem; lily flower, duck; pig; Hathor head (strung with disc beads), seven figures of deities including Shu and Sekhmet; fourteen plain hedgehog scaraboids, severally of green pinkish and yellow glaze, apparently from one mould; two elongated barrel beads of dark brown and brown and white paste, and one of yellow glass? (originally dark blue?) with green herringbone; a smaller one of green glaze; some dark red ring beads; blue glaze heart; bronze thin, shell-like pendant; hollow drop earring, now containing alabaster penannular ring; remains of two rings of bronze and one of iron; short nail-like object of lead with flat round head and flat shank; spoon of fine hard greenish paste of good work but imperfect, the handle in shape of an Asiatic bringing the bowl as tribute on his shoulders, the bowl inscribed "May Bubastis open a good year", a New Year's gift (the handle has been broken off anciently below the waist, the hanging drapery also broken off short, and a large chip lost of the bowl); three discs of shell, d. nearly 2, not pierced, edges slightly sloping, the smaller faces of two darker, with traces of green-stained cement, probably therefore for inlay in bronze; flat square of ivory about 1.2; shell of Nerita crassilabrum, a ball bead of calcite, another of cornelian.

> 11. Rect. ; ext. Many beads, shells, etc., on body, heap of ornaments on right of legs ; from which, toilet spoon XXXI, 5, bronze shell XL, 3, hedgehog beads LVI, 31, bird LVII, 3, glaze and glass barrel beads LXIV, 15. (Bn.)

* * *

Bearing in mind that the excavation was done in a very short time and documented by only two people, it is astonishing how detailed the descriptions and sketches are. But looking in depth at the tomb cards, we have to consider some problems which reduce the validity of any research on the cemetery of Sanam.

–The visual documentation is very poor: only a few photographs were done in the field, thus we have few pictures of the tombs themselves.

–In about two thirds of the descriptions, the measurements of the tomb are not given.

–In some cases, the written description of a tomb's appearance cannot be connected with the form drawn in the plan.

–The descriptions given of skeletons are poor. In 338 cases the length of the skeleton is given, but lack clear indications of sex and age.

–The finds are occasionally described in detail, but mostly only summarily. This is particularly problematic when dealing with the engraved scarabs.

–The descriptions of the pottery are given only in their type-form, for which schematic line-drawings exist. Some of the types cannot be distinguished accurately from the given measurements and line drawings.

I.4.3. The publication of F. Ll. Griffith

Since the First World War began immediately after the excavation, Griffith was unable to publish the results of the whole Oxford Excavations in Nubia until after the end of war. In 1922 the publication of the temple and the treasury was presented in the *Liverpool Annals of Archaeology and Anthropology*, and the publication of the cemetery followed one year later in the same journal.

Looking through the original documentation, it is obvious that only part of the descriptions, photographs and sketches were published. To visualise the difference even of published tombs, I present the entry for tomb 0011 in the tomb cards and in the publication (fig. 3).

I.4.4. Research on the cemetery of Sanam after Griffith

Since Sanam is the largest known non-royal cemetery of the Napatan Period, it is clearly important for any research on Napatan tombs, especially in order to find parallels or differences with other cemeteries. Publications of more recent excavations of Napatan cemeteries such as Qustul (Williams 1990) or Missiminia (Vila 1980) always correlate their own results with the cemetery of Sanam. Moreover, there are some detailed studies on several object categories, which are present at Sanam also. For example, objects from Sanam are included in the book on representations of gods in the National Museum of Khartoum by Eleonora Kormysheva (2006). And finally, I have already published some specific objects from the site.[4]

It is a pity that my funding did not enable research on the original objects, which in some instances have still to be located, as well as described, photographed and drawn. Thus, this investigation is based on the documentation of Griffith stored in the Griffith Institute. The tomb cards were entered into a database, the ink-drawn plan scanned and redone for publication. Finally, I was able to study all of the photographs, some of which are published here for the first time.

[4] Lohwasser 2002a, 2002b, 2006a, 2006b, 2007, 2010, forthcoming.

II. The archaeology of the cemetery of Sanam

II.1. Description of different tombs and burials

In the following section, I will describe and show photographs of some of the tombs in the cemetery. The tombs selected are intended to provide an overview of the different burial types. The reader should gain an impression of their variety, ranging from bricked as well as sand burials, with extended and contracted bodies, empty and well furnished graves. In the following chapters, I will refer to these descriptions. The text is a rewritten copy of the tomb cards of Griffith. In the brackets after the tomb-number Griffith sometimes includes an abbreviation for the museum to which he distributed the object(s).

Fig. 4: Grave 1162 (photo: Griffith-Institute)

Bricked grave with extended burial with cartonnage (fig. 4):

1162 was rectangular and lined with bricks (280 by 145, int. 240 by 40; D. c. 40 cm). The chamber was arched. The arch started at 25cm. There were two skeletons of adults in this chamber, extended and with the hands on the pelvis, the head was oriented towards the river. The remains of a cartonnage mask were found on the southern skeleton. Its face was red and the wig white and blue with some red.

Fig. 5: Grave 0485 (photo: Griffith-Institute)

Bricked grave with extended burial and few objects (fig. 5):

0485 (Ashmolean) was a bricked grave of rather irregular shape, carved into the soft gebel (exterior: 2.4 m long and 1.05 wide; interior: 2.15 x 0.5 m. It was 0.6 m high). There was found a small skeleton, about 1.5 m long, extended on its back with the hands resting on the pelvis. The head was oriented towards the river. At the left side of the skull was found ram-headed scarabs with free legs, most likely depicting Amun. It has an oval base made of bronze which is inscribed. There was also found a rectangular green glazed plaque with Nile god

Fig. 6: Grave 0521 (photo: Griffith-Institute)

Sand burials with contracted persons and no objects (fig. 6):

There are many tombs with no or few objects and where the body was just placed into the ground. In 0521 was found a small skeleton in a contracted position placed on its left side. The heels are near the hips and the hands positioned in front of and touching the face. Two barrel beads were the only grave goods. 0521A was found just north of it. Again it contained a small skeleton, extended on the back. The hands were on the pelvis and the head oriented towards the river.

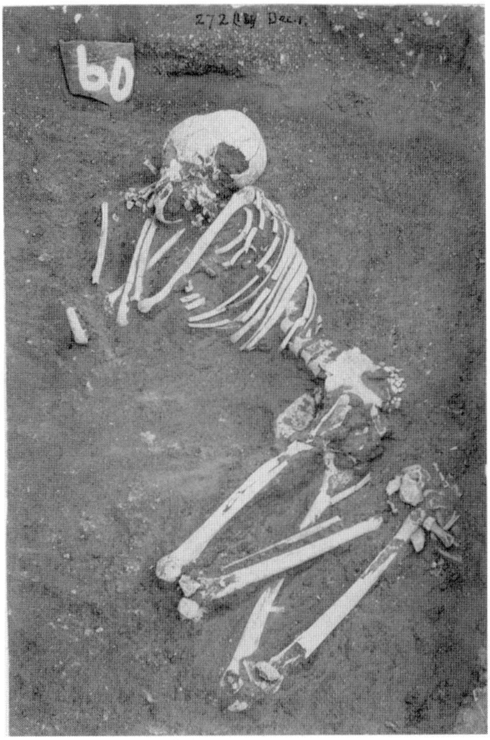

Fig. 7: Grave 0060 (photo: Griffith-Institute)

Oval shaft with contracted burial and few objects (fig. 7):

0060 (Munich) This is a shallow oval grave in the gebel, without brick lining. It was found to contain a small skeleton, loosely contracted on the right side, with hands to face. Behind the pelvis, were four greenish and four yellowish glazed barrel beads, and one whitish ball bead. The excavation also found two coarse greenish glaze beads, one of them melon shaped, and a large number of broad ring beads of whitish glaze, "with shell of *Oliva inflate*," according to the excavation record. The order of the beads uncertain, but several of the ring beads were together on the string.

Fig. 8: Grave 0143 (photo: Griffith-Institute)

Rectangular shaft with contracted burial and rich equipment (fig. 8):
0143 (Brussels) This grave consisted of a rectangular trench 230 by 95

cm, cut in the gebel with rounded corners. It contained the skeleton of an adult, loosely contracted on the right side. The left hand was on the pelvis, while the right one was before the face. Behind the head was found a large two-handled pot, of coarse, red clay and on the inside blackish. It was hand-made and the mouth was decorated with zig-zag impressions. The pot was covered by cup (h. 13 cm, dm 13.5 cm) of thin micaceous hand-made red ware, black inside and on the rim. At the elbow lay a coarse hand-made cup with a red rim, 13 cm high and with a diameter of 13.5-14.5 cm. In the lap were discovered similar cups and one more cup was placed at the knee (12 cm high, 14 cm diameter). There was also a thin wheel-made pot of reddish ware with buff painted surface (16 cm high, 17 cm wide). It seemed to have been pierced at the bottom. At the feet was a further cup. In front of the left hand was found a small piece of galena with a quartz pebble as palette, bruised on one face. From the back of the head down the cheek, there was a double string of yellow and green glaze openwork udjats. Round the neck were still preserved two strings of beads and pendants: one of Hathor-head pendants, separated by tiny ring beads, arranged yellow-red-yellow (sometimes yellow-red only); and a second string of mixed beads, the larger ones separated by ring-beads in the order yellow-black-yellow the larger form here included a cylinder engraved with a nefer hieroglyphic sign, carnelian, melon, and ball beads, small glazed frogs, amethyst ball bead and a steatite udjat-eye. Below the armpit of the right arm, there was a string of small disc beads and several groups of beads of different sizes; including two glazed flower pendants and a pierced yellow and reddish pebble pendant. Probably around the upper arm were four steatite scarabs, two repaired with glaze and three steatite beads. At the right heel was a small *conus* shell. Furthermore, there were many small open-work udjats of green and yellow glaze and glaze and shell beads; there was also a small carnelian pendant resembling a circular seal with a straight handle.

Fig. 9: Grave 0034 (photo: Griffith-Institute)

Tomb 0034 (fig. 9) is an irregular shaft with an extended skeleton and pottery equipment:

The grave shaft is carved into the gebel, tapering towards the bottom, 210 cm by 100-40 cm, D. 100 cm and with rounded end. In the north half there is a skeleton. It is extended on its back with its left hand on the pelvis, the right hand down the side of the body, while the head is fallen to left. On right of the skull is a jar of pink hard ware, wheel made, IIIa. The outside is whitish. It is 5 cm high. There is also a tumbler, wheel made, exterior bright red, burnished, rim painted red inside. It is 11.6 cm high, with a diameter at the mouth of 7.6-8.2 cm, the bottom is pierced. The third vessel is a red tumbler of similar ware but not burnished (15.5 cm high, with a diameter of 12.5-13.5 cm).

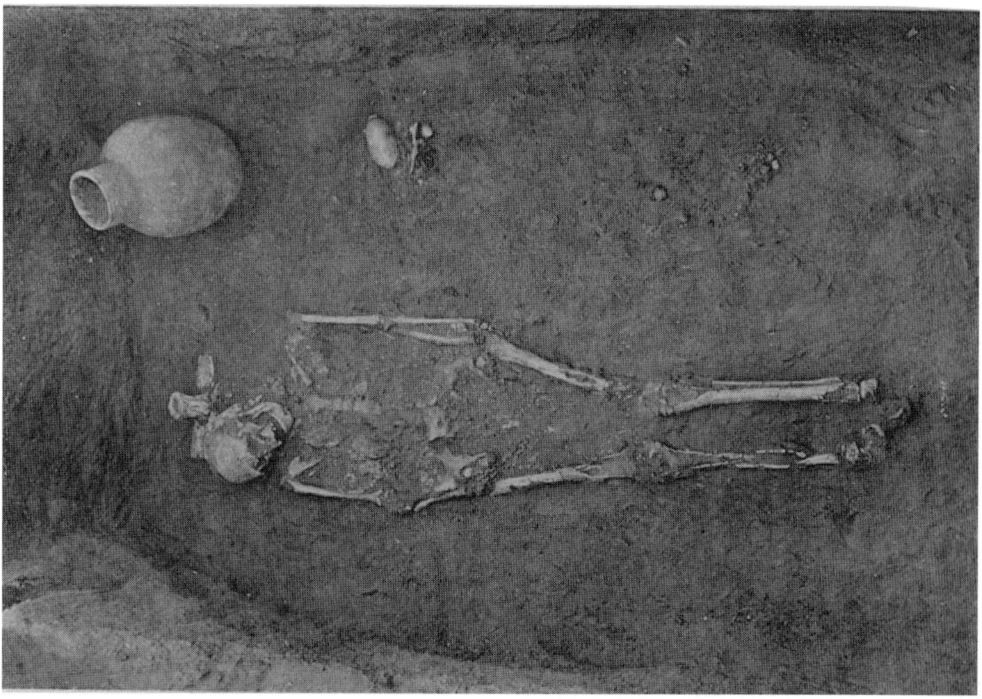

Fig. 10: Grave 0963 (photo: Griffith-Institute)

Bricked grave with extended skeleton and rich equipment, including a headrest (fig. 10):

Grave 0963 (Ashmolean): This is a rectangular bricked grave in firm sand, the interior is 230 by 110 cm. Towards the south side there is a skeleton of an adult, extended on its back. The hands are on the pelvis, while the head is orientated towards river. The skeleton is 153 cm long. There are remains of network and beadcloth. Behind the head there is an ivory headrest, much decayed, with a rectangular base (23 x 6 cm) and with a square in middle for support of the pillar. The pillar is 7 cm high and oval in section widening at the top and bottom. A fragment of one side of the curved rest remains. At the north end of the west wall there is a red jar, 37 cm high and 23 cm wide. Inside the mouth of a wheel-made beaker of reddish ware, painted red on outside and on mouth inside, as XIb, H. 14,5, D. 8,6-8,1, bottom broken through with large hole (intentionally?). Near the north wall, opposite the elbow there is an alabastron, but it looks unpierced and the neck is straight (11.2 cm high). There is a toilet spoon in the shape of a swimming girl of yellowish faience, holding a rectangular tray in her outstretched arms; her hair is black and tied with a yellow fillet in a bunch behind the head (see fig. 41). There is a string hole on either side of the tray, between the arms. Indication of anklets carved in relief. It is 11 cm long. Beneath the figure are the remains of an iron object; nearby a mussel shell. At the east end of the north wall was found a frog of clear chalcedony with brown bands. There is a small ball bead of chalcedony, one of carnelian and a small glazed udjat-eye in a rectangle. In the filling of the grave is a drop bead of green feldspar, and a similar one of amethyst, a carnelian ball bead, small udjat-eye, a serrated lentoid bead and many ring beads of bluish glaze.

Lateral niche grave with contracted burial and rich equipment (fig. 11): 1038 (Berlin). This is a grave with lateral niche to north and a shelf to the

Fig. 11: Grave 1038 (photo: Griffith-Institute)

south. The grave is 2 m long and has an opening of about 160 cm. Two skeletons of adults were found, superposed. The upper one of a woman, placed in a contracted position on left side with the right hand on the chest. The left hand placed on the forehead. The head is orientated towards the river. The lower skeleton contracted on its right side with head again towards the river. Behind the upper part of the head is a red-mouthed bowl. It is 15 cm high with a diameter of 17 cm. It was found broken and rotten. There is a bronze mirror which is almost circular, measuring 19.3 by 20.1 cm. Marks of cloth were found on one face. On the mirror is a string of shell disc beads. A string of short cylindrical beads of white quartz, alternating with glass beads of similar shape at the western edge of the mirror. All were found decayed. There was also a round mirror, a pair of penannular bronze wire earrings, which are corroded together and a ribbed penannular bead of red paste. There is a cowroid of the same material with 2 Amun ram's heads; a hedgehog of green glaze, a burnt steatite rectangular plaque with cynocephalus. A kind of herringbone decoration (*asplenium* leaves) is engraved on the sides. Beside the mirror on the north side, is a large udjat-eye of blue glaze turned green, its pupil and brow black, and a ball bead of greenish glaze. Beneath the mirror was found a large lentoid bead of white quartz, flattened below, W. 1.9 cm and a cylindrical bead of the same material. Finally there is a small carnelian ball bead.

Rectangular bricked grave, extended burial, many alabastra, possibly stored in a box or bag (fig. 12):

0430 (Khartoum): This is a rectangular bricked grave in the sand, one brick thick, inside 200 by 75 cm wide with a remaining depth of 60 cm (without vault) axis 300. There is an adult skeleton extended on back with its head towards the river. The burial is disturbed. Behind the head there is small alabstron about 3.8 cm high, a second alabastron with a lost neck and remaining 7 cm high, another one is broken and 8 cm high, there are two others, one 6.9 and the other 7.0 cm high. Perhaps from the neck there is a turquoise glazed sistrum with a papyrus stem, sow, there is a kneeling Shu, an Isis with Horus, a left hand, an udjat-eye, a silver barrel bead, a drop of basalt. They are all of fair workmanship. Around the waist there is a string of carnelian barrel beads with one very large and one smaller flattened barrel bead of lapis. At the left hip or hand there is a small ribbed alabastron of thin green glaze. In the south-east corner is a miniature amphora of the same shape. Its neck is formed by a cylindrical glass bead, which when found was already decayed. There is also a delicately shaped pomegranate bead of the same glaze.

Fig. 12: Grave 0430 (photo: Griffith-Institute)

II.2. The tombs

Griffith located 1619 tombs in the cemetery, most of which were excavated. He decided not to excavate some cave graves which were damaged or in danger of collapse.

II.2.1. Tomb marker

Griffith (1923: 75) found no trace of tomb superstructures. Nevertheless, we have to assume that there was some kind of tomb marker, since only a few – according to the size and density of the cemetery – were cut through by another tomb. On the other hand, many tombs were re-opened to insert one or several more burials. But since some tombs were built very close to each other, especially in the crowded central area, we have to imagine that there were no monumental superstructures.

We do not know the form of these assumed superstructures. The tumulus, the typical Nubian superstructure of all periods and all regions, is possible as well as the pyramid, the superstructure of the royal and elite burials of the Napatan period in El Kurru, Nuri and Meroe. We expect a sand tumulus would erode quickly, especially over the sand burials, since there are often several skeletons buried one on top of another. The vault over the staircase and over rectangular bricked tombs may also have functioned as a domed superstructure. There is no evidence that the vaults were covered by soil, and so they may have been visible above the ground. Last but not least we may imagine fans or poles with signs serving as the markers of recent burials. We do not know about chapels either. Some offering tables were found near the entrance of tombs, but all of them seem to be in secondary positions.[5]

---

[5] For evidence of the funerary cult in Sanam see chapter IV.2.

II.2.2. Orientation of the tombs

Most of the graves are orientated 280°-310° (north-west). A few tombs of each type are orientated in other directions, especially the sand burials which present a great variety (fig. 13). This is maybe influenced by the fact that Griffith could not give a precise axis of the tomb, since there is no architectural feature with sand burials. There he measured the longitudinal axis of each burial, which may have caused the variations.

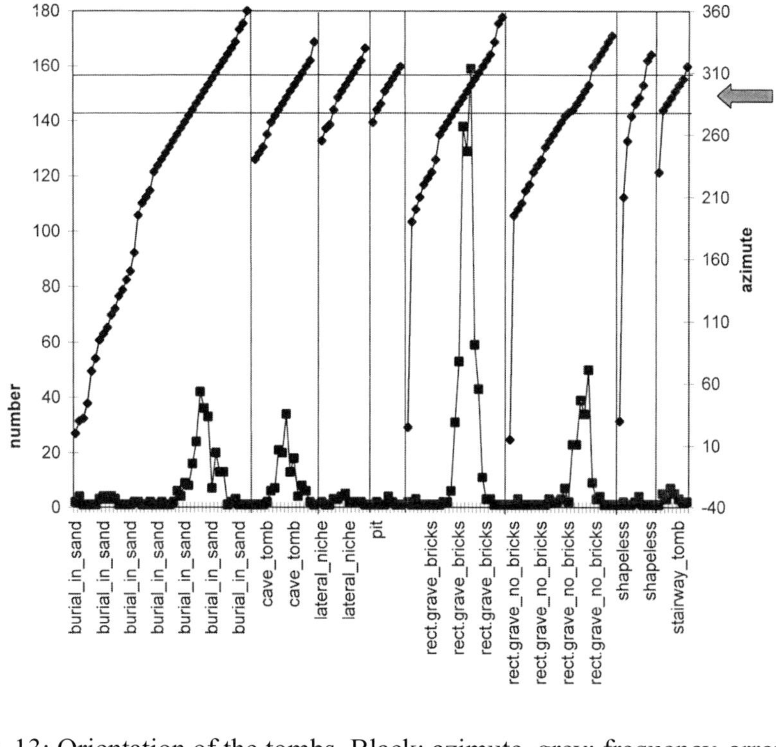

Fig. 13: Orientation of the tombs. Black: azimute, grey: frequency, arrow: region of the most common orientations

1176 tombs have an axis between 280° and 310°, which is the normal orientation to the Nile. 1348 tombs have an axis between 260° and 330°, which may be also interpreted as orientation towards the Nile. Some of the tombs may have been orientated in relation to stars, some to other tombs.

II.2.3. Dimensions of the tombs

Tomb size naturally varies between the different types, but also within one type. Griffith seldom gives measurements enabling the tomb's size to be calculated, thus it is not possible to present here a detailed analysis of the variations in their dimensions. Nevertheless we should distinguish

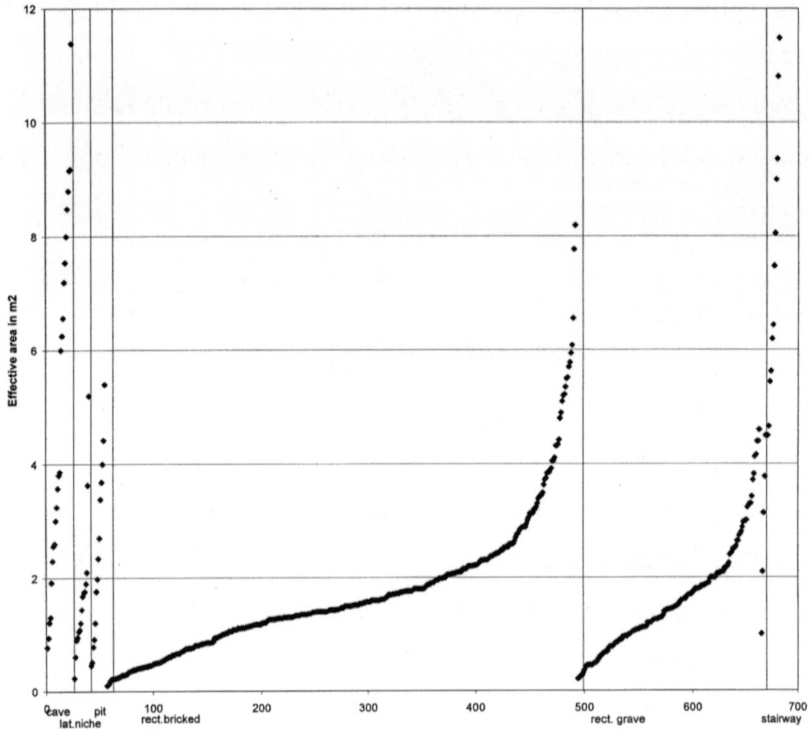

Fig. 14: Effective area in m^{2}, break down into grave types

between the overall area of each tomb – which includes the outlying walls as well as staircases – and the effective area, which is the available area for the burial proper. For 275 tombs Griffith gave both measurements, the surrounding wall and the inner space. In bricked tombs, one can expect about 50-70% of the whole covered area for the burial. Cave graves and stairway tombs less (35-65%), since staircases and entrance constructions are not part of the burial space. It is interesting to note that the number of stairs and the depth of the grave do not vary in relation to the size of the space.

We know the effective area of 684 tombs. 80% are small, with an inner space up to 2.5 m^2. 6.3% are very large, their inner space is up to 4.5 m^2 (fig. 14).

II.2.4. Tomb types

Griffith (1923: 76-79) defined the tomb types A-H:

A: Cave graves with stairway approach

B: Built graves with stairway approach

C: Rectangular pit, lined with bricks and with a brick roof

D: Shallow rectangular trench

E: Narrow graves with or without bricked sides tapered to the foot end

F: Lateral niche graves

G: Shallow oval and indeterminate graves and burials in sand

H: Two shapeless unlined graves with a few bricks laid diagonally

I modified the types according to the descriptions in the tomb cards and define four categories:

1.cave graves

2.tombs with brick structures, these include rectangular bricked as well as staircase tombs

3.shaft tombs, which have round, oval, rectangular or irregular shafts as well as lateral niche graves – all these tombs lack any brick structure

4.sand graves, where the burial is interred directly into the sand without an architectural feature which could be called tomb

These categories are subdivided in types.

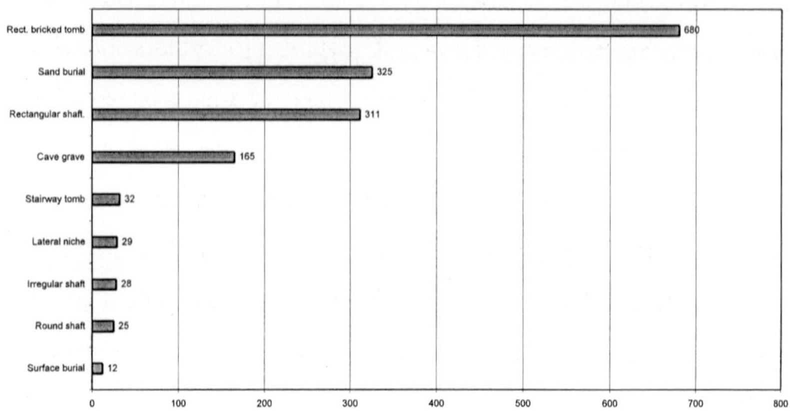

Fig. 15: Frequency of grave types

The 1619 tombs in the cemetery comprise (fig. 15):

680 rectangular bricked tombs (42 %)

325 sand burials (20%)

311 rectangular shaft graves (19 %)

165 cave graves (at least 36 of them with more than one chamber)(10%)

32 stairway tombs (3 with two chambers) (1.9 %)

29 lateral niche graves (1.8 %)

28 irregular shafts (1.7%)

25 round shafts (1.5 %)

12 surface burials, no grave type to trace (0.7 %)

The rest are destroyed or unfinished tombs.

Cave graves (Fig. 16, 22)

Since cave graves are restricted to the gebel area, they are found only in the southeast and southwest sectors of the cemetery. They are dug into the ground; access to the burial is via stairs or, seldom, by ramps. The subterranean chambers are roughly hewn out and left unsmoothed and undecorated. Since they did not use columns or pillars, some of the chambers have collapsed. 35 of the graves of this type could not be excavated because they were already destroyed or were in danger of collapse. 85 cave graves have one subterranean chamber, 19 two, 5 three and 12 four rooms. Maybe the regular cave grave had four rooms, one in the centre, one axial and two lateral chambers on either side. Construction started with the axial chamber followed by the lateral chambers. Since only five tombs had three rooms with only one lateral chamber it is reasonable to assume that these were unfinished.

Fig. 16: Cave grave 0001 (photo: Griffith-Institute)

The number of steps leading to the chambers varies from one to 20. In front of the entrance, a small platform may have been used for ritual activities. Most of the cave graves were robbed entirely, thus we cannot be sure about the predominant burial position. However, all of the 39 documented skeletons were laid down in an extended position. One secondary burial was found in a semi-contracted position. In my opinion, cave graves with more than one subterranean room were already built in the New Kingdom.[6] The single-roomed cave graves are to be dated to the Napatan period, since apart from the architecture, the finds are also Napatan. Since stairways are introduced in the time of Piye, we should date these graves in Sanam to the reign of Piye at earliest. Cave graves were reopened several times and include multiple burials. Even the only documented Meroitic burials are secondary interments in cave graves.

[6] Lohwasser 2010.

Tombs with bricking

The stairway tombs as well as the rectangular bricked tombs are surrounded by unfired mud bricks. They consist of rectangular built walls and a vaulted roof. The covering of the small tombs consist of two rows of inclined bricks. Since the burial is inserted from the east, the east wall was the last to be finished. This wall was predetermined to be reopened again.

The tombs with bricking can be arranged in two types according to their entrance design. Stairway tombs have a stairway leading to the burial chamber, in only two instances is there a ramp.

Stairway tombs (fig. 17, 23)

This type consists of a large open shaft, outlined with bricks and vaulted. A staircase leading down to the burial is sometimes covered by bricks. It

Fig. 17: Stairway tomb 1428 (photo: Griffith-Institute)

seems that this type of grave follows the cave grave type, but is used in areas of the cemetery where there is no gebel, or at least where the soil is too weak or too sandy to support a cave grave. Stairway tombs are located in a narrow band in the middle of the cemetery, near and interweaving with the cave graves.

Some of the tombs are quite small (4-5 m^2), others are big (up to 31 m^2); these are the largest tombs in the cemetery. Like the cave graves, there was very often more than one burial (up to 12 skeletons) lying extended on their backs.

This type of tomb architecture seems to be a local form, since up to now it is not known from any other Napatan cemetery. Three of the stairway tombs have two chambers; all of them differ in their layout and size.[7]

These graves are situated mostly in the north and west of the cemetery, with only a few in the south. Most are small, only a small number had an internal space of up to 7 m^2. According to Griffith, the upper part of these tombs is lined with bricks or the tomb is entirely built of bricks. The roof consists of a bricked vault or at least of two bricks put together standing upright.

As with the aforementioned tombs, rectangular bricked tombs also contained multiple burials. It is not sure whether the secondary burials were interred from the east wall – the last one erected – or by opening the roof again.

[7] Graves 0036, 0089 and 1619, (see Griffith 1923: 78)

Fig. 18: Bricked tomb 1110 (photo: Griffith-Institute)

Rectangular bricked tombs (Fig. 18, 24, see also fig. 5)

Most of the burials are documented lying extended on their backs. We know of comparable tombs in the north of the empire (Missiminia), but none of them are documented from Meroe. Maybe the construction of bricked tombs was restricted to areas without stable soil. Indeed, in Meroe the construction of shaft tombs was possible without danger of collapse.

Shaft tombs (Fig. 25)

These are simple shafts cut into the gebel; this type is seldom constructed in the sandy area. Their form varies from round to oval or rectangular, and some of them were also called irregular by Griffith. The rare lateral niche tombs can be regarded as special types of shaft tombs.

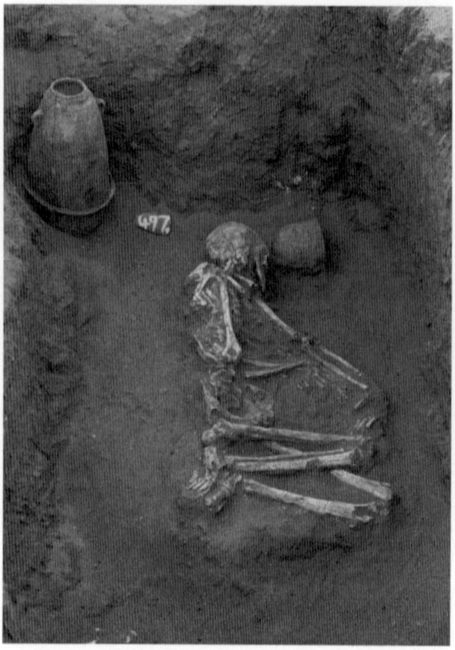

Fig. 19: Shaft tomb 0497 (photo: Griffith-Institute)

Rectangular shaft tombs (fig. 19, see also fig. 8)

These graves are situated in the south and central part of the cemetery, with only a few in the north.

The graves are shafts without any preserved brick work. Griffith suggested that since there were no traces of roof constructions, the corpse was directly covered by the sand. However, also in this type of grave there were secondary burials that could only be intruded through the opening. In some instances there are two burials on the same level, and so these had to be buried at the same time, if we accept the suggestion of Griffith. In other cemeteries big stone slabs covered the entrance of the shaft. This might have also happened in Sanam, although no slabs were found. Since the area is poor of hard stone, these slabs might have been reused in the construction of buildings.

Most of the rectangular shaft tombs are small (up to 2 m^2), only a few of them had greater internal dimensions of up to 4.6 m^2. Griffith (1923: 85) suggested that these tombs are earlier in date.

More than half of the documented skeletons were buried in a (semi-) contracted position.

Round shaft tombs (see fig. 7)

Some simple round or oval shaft tombs are situated in the southern part of the cemetery, very few are found in the north. Twenty of them are described as oval, four as round and one as triangular. On the plan of the cemetery nevertheless, most of them are drawn rectangular.

This kind of shaft tomb is attested in Nubia especially in the earlier periods, however for Napatan times the evidence is very scare. The burials are mostly (semi-)contracted.

Irregular shafts (see fig. 9)

Griffith described some graves as shapeless or indeterminate as well as irregular. I summarised all of them as irregular. Maybe these tombs are eroded rectangular or round shafts.

Lateral niche graves (Fig. 20, 26, see also fig. 11)

In a few shafts there is a small lateral niche which housed the corpse. In 11 instances the niche is in the north wall, in 7 in the south wall. For 8

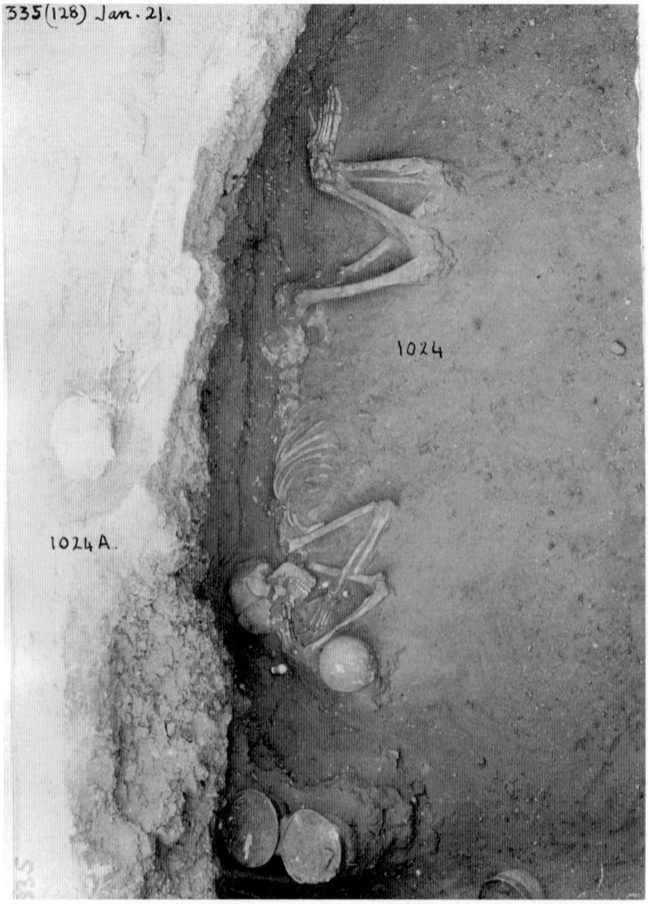

Fig. 20: Lateral niche tomb 1024 (photo: Griffith-Institute)

graves, Griffith did not document the wall which had the niche. The graves are situated in two groups in the southwest and in the central part of the cemetery, only one tomb is in the north. The lateral niche type ivery often used in Napatan cemeteries, but they seem to be restricted to the north of the empire, as none was excavated in the region of Meroe. Since this type covers only 1.8% in the large cemetery of Sanam, seldom occurs in El Kurru, and never in Nuri, the region of the Jebel Barkal may form the transitional area.

Most of the burials are extended on their backs, but there are also some documented as contracted on their sides.

Sand graves (Fig. 21, 27, see also fig. 6)

Simple pits in the loose sand are situated in the north of the cemetery. The corpse was laid in and covered with sand, maybe a sand tumulus formed a tomb marking. These are not tombs with an architectural aspect, but simply covered burials. It is likely that many of these graves were eroded and not discovered by Griffith.

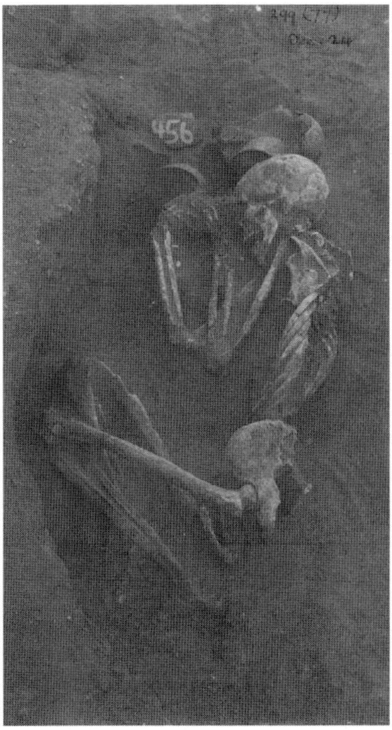

Fig. 21: Sand burial 0456 (photo: Griffith-Institute)

Since Griffith defined the tomb's axis according to the direction of the skeleton's spine, there are considerable anomalies with this type. Most of the non-Nile axis is directed towards the east.

Sand burials are situated in the sandy area of the cemetery – in the north as well as on higher levels in the southeast. Since sand burials are restricted to a sandy underground, they are not used in cemeteries with hard soil only, like Missiminia or Qustul. Maybe the cleft burials of the rocky area of the 2nd and 4th cataract are equivalent to the Sanam sand burials: in neither case was there a tomb structure, while in both cases the corpse is laid down and covered with the surrounding material.

Most sand graves contained only one burial, some two, but seldom more. Since the secondary burials are found in a higher level above the existing ones, one can assume that the tomb markings vanished very quickly and the new burials were made without knowledge of the existing burials.

In about a quarter of the graves the burials were in a (semi)contracted position, the other burials are extended.

Special forms

Some very eroded graves were called surface burials or simply burials by Griffith, because he could not trace the type of the grave. Very few rectangular bricked tombs had a coffin-like shape with a broad and a narrower end. And at last three tombs had holes to hold the grave goods, which was very common in Missiminia.

Animal burials

Four tombs housed animal burials, three of them were lions and one had two fishes. Two of the lions were adorned with faience beads and an amulet, one of the fishes had an iron blade still resting in his body.

Fig. 22: Distribution of cave graves

Fig. 23: Distribution of stairway tombs

Fig. 24: Distribution of bricked tombs

Fig. 25: Distribution of shaft tombs

Fig. 26: Distribution of lateral niche tombs

Fig. 27: Distribution of sand burials

II.3. The burials

Griffith recorded 1560 skeletons in the cemetery of Sanam, and 278 graves where he found no bones.

In general, there was only one burial per grave. Some tombs where more than one burial is documented is evidence that they had been opened more than once.

In a few instances it seems that a tomb was used for a secondary deposition of skeletons, such as grave 0324: "a confusion of sks. (17 skulls)" or 0728: "On the SW corner, almost at the height of the top of the roof, confused remains of sks. piled up."

From this table (fig. 28) we can see clearly that in general single burials were laid in the sand and multiple burials were common in cave and stairway tombs. Also, rectangular bricked graves were reopened several times, but shafts less often. There is no clear relation between large space and multiple burials – sometimes in large tombs just one person was buried while some small tombs contained more than one.

Type	Number of burials	Frequency
Cave grave	1	35
	2	12
	3	3
	4	1
	5	1
	6	3
	8	1
Stairway tomb	1	7
	2	8
	4	1
	5	2
	6	1

	12	1
Rectangular bricked tomb	1	330
	2	60
	3	20
	4	13
	5	9
	6	4
	7	4
	8	1
	12	2
	13	1
	17	1
Rectangular shaft	1	157
	2	26
	3	5
	4	4
Round shaft	1	14
	2	2
	4	2
	9	1
Irregular shaft	1	19
	2	3
	3	1
Lateral niche	1	18
	2	1
Sand burial	1	302
	2	15
	3	4
	4	1
	5	1

Fig 28: Number of individuals, reflected in tomb types

II.3.1. Positions

All in all, Griffith documented 163 contracted (K, 14.6%), 76 semi contracted (S, 6.8%) and 878 extended (G, 78.8%) skeletons.

When we combine contracted and semi contracted to "not extended" and the grave types to the categories, caves, bricked tombs, shaft tombs and sand burials, it is very clear that in the shaft burials the "not extended" position is dominant, in the other categories the extended position is more common (fig. 29).

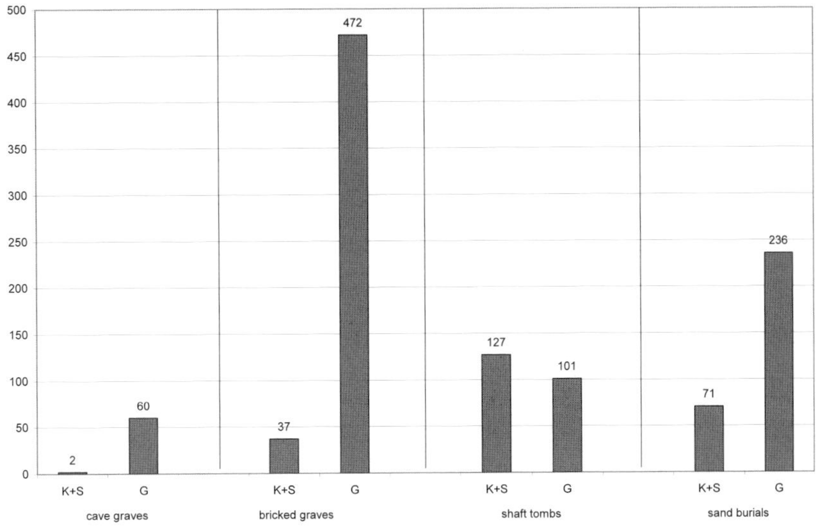

Fig 29: Distribution of burial poses according to grouped grave types

Extended position (see for example figs. 3, 4, 5, 6, 9, 10, 12)

The extended skeletons are laid on their backs with the face up to the sky, their hands rest on their hips or femur. Only in two instances in sand burials were the hands turned up to the face.

Contracted position (see for example figs. 6, 7, 8, 11)

The contracted skeletons lay on their right or left side, the body is bent and the legs contracted to the belly. Only in five cases was the skeleton found contracted on its back, but this seems to be a result of disturbance. The hands are positioned in front of the face, but seldom folded under the head. In few cases, the hands are placed on the legs.

There is no difference in the occurrence of the right (94 x) or left (98 x) position; their distribution in the area of the cemetery, as well as on grave types and the different ages of individuals is more or less indifferent.

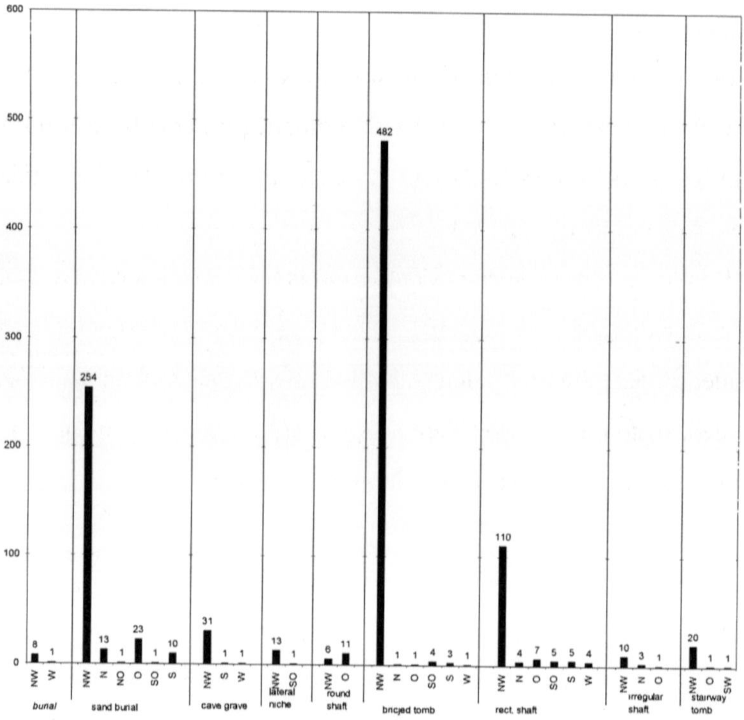

Fig. 30: Orientation of the burials according to grave types

Burial positions in other Napatan cemeteries

Most burials in other Napatan cemeteries are interred in the extended position. Only seldom do we find contracted skeletons, most are of small children in the cemetery at Missiminia or sporadic examples in round pits in Kerma.[8] In Tombos only women are buried in the contracted position.[9] In Qustul, El Kurru, Nuri and Meroe bed burials were found.[10] They are absent in Missiminia and Sanam, but since in the latter no wood was conserved, we cannot be sure that this custom did not exist there.

II.3.2. Orientation of the skeletons

In most instances the head of the skeletons is directed towards the Nile, i.e. north-west. Griffith documented anomalies especially in sand graves and in round pits. There are some more skeletons orientated towards east, seldom towards north (fig. 30).

As it is to be expected, most of the anomalies in orientation were found with non-extended positions. In general, we can say that 95% of the extended burials are orientated towards the Nile, but only 69% of the non-extended. In some cases the skeletons might be orientated towards another grave, but it seems to be a very seldom occurrence.

II.3.3. Age and sex of the dead

Griffith (1923: 81) states that the fragile skeletons did not permit an investigation of their sex or a more precise age. The anthropologist Armand Ruffer was in Sanam for a few days, but his report is missing. Griffith gave an estimation about the sex of 31 skeletons. He described 12 individuals as male, mostly if the length of their skeleton was more than 170 cm. 19 Skeletons he explained to be female, mostly with newborn at their side.

For 792 burials he estimated the age using the categories of adult (549,

[8] Vila 1980a: 26, Bonnet 1999: 4.
[9] Smith 2003: 198-199.
[10] Williams 1990: 13, Dunham 1950: 131–132; Dunham 1955: 18, Adams 1977: 280.

69.4%), young (69, 8.7%), child (98, 12.4%), infant (75, 9.4%) and one foetus, but he never defined the categories. Neither the place in the cemetery nor the grave type or burial position shows a clear preference by any of the age groups. Only according to the grave goods can we see differences: adults use more vessels (pottery, stone, faience, bronze), while children are provided with more amulets.

II.3.4. Ethnic description

There is hardly any chance of finding any ethnic membership for the skeletons. In 338 cases Griffith gave the length of the skeleton; the average is about 140-160 cm. There are some very tall skeletons of 180-190 cm, which means that when alive these individuals must have been between 190 and 200 cm tall! But considering the study of Mukherjee, Rao und Trevor on the Jebel Moya skeletons, there is no possibility to link them to the tall Nilotic people.[11] Thus we have to accept that in Sanam a small number of very tall individuals were buried, who maybe descendants from a different ethnic group to the rest of the population.

II.4. The finds

II.4.1. Introduction

In 825 of the 1619 graves of the cemetery Griffith documented finds – decoration of the body, grave goods and items of funerary rituals. As a source, I had the description of Griffith only. I was able to investigate the objects of Sanam in the museums of Berlin, Leiden and Brussels, but not those stored in the National Museum Khartoum, Ashmolean Museum Oxford, Pitt-Rivers Museum Oxford, Fitzwilliam Museum Cambridge, Bolton Museum, Manchester Museum, Brighton Museum, British

[11] Mukherjee/ Rao/ Trevor 1955: 89-90.

1 Incense burner

2 Bead net (grave 0179)

3 Decorated solid earring of faience (grave 1062)

4 Sewing plaque (?) (grave 1095)

5 Two more elaborated beads

6 Several tone beads

7 Barrel beads with painted decoration (grave 1516)

8 Various beads (modern strung, grave 0663)

9 Various beads (modern strung, grave 0015A)

10 Poppy pendants of carnelian (grave 0231)

11 Fish-and-flower-pendant (grave 1062)

12 Necklace with amulets and beads (grave 0337), modern strung

13 Udjats from faience and jaspis (graves 0714, 0120)

14 Udjat in openwork (grave 0722)

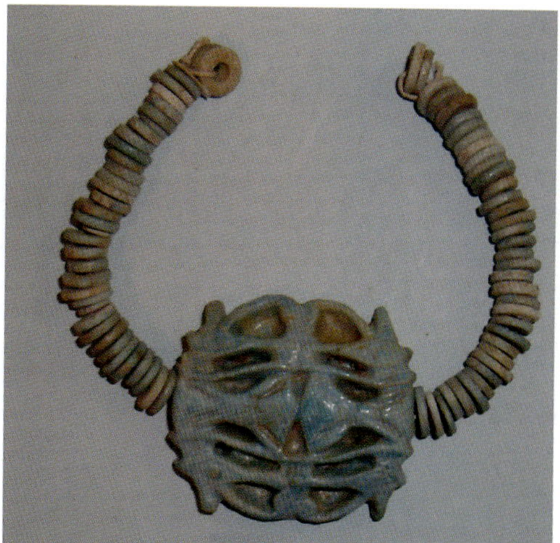

15 Quadruple-udjat (grave 1516)

16 Amulet-plaques of Khonsu (grave 0722)

17 Frog (grave 1516)

18 Decorated pot (grave 218)

19 Napatan pot (grave 0143)

20 Alabastron (grave 0337)

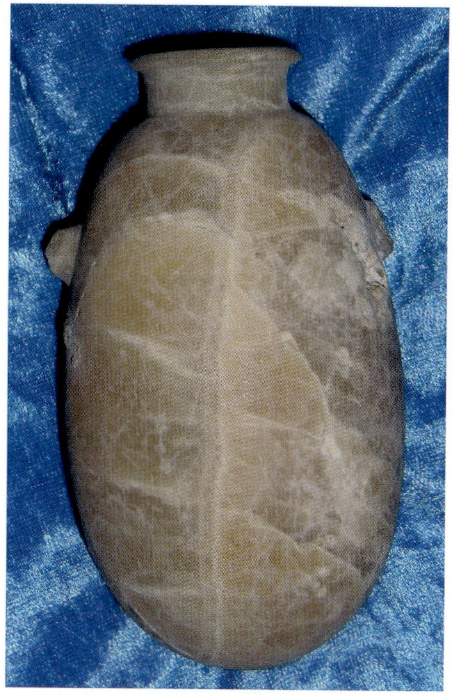

21 Alabastron (grave 0337)

22 Mirror (grave 0632)

23 Jug from the Mediterranean (grave 1416)

24 Plaque (grave 1516)

25 Plaque (grave 1516)

Museum London, Petrie Museum London, Egyptian Museum Munich and Antikenmuseum Basel. Today, some additional objects have proved difficult to trace, since they were offered to private collections.

In some cases Griffith wrote very detailed descriptions of the finds, but for others he gave only summaries of the inventories ("scarabs etc."). A complete investigation of the finds from the cemetery would be a helpful project and might change some of the results in this book.

II.4.2. "Empty" graves *(see for example the sand burials fig. 6)*

758 graves lacked any finds. However, as 39 cave graves were not excavated due to danger of their collapse, and a sizeable number of graves were plundered, which might account for their lack of funerary goods, we have to consider the unplundered graves only (fig. 31).

Type	**number of tombs without finds**	**Percent of tombs without finds (%)**	**Percent of this type in the whole cemetery (%)**
Cvae grave	-	-	10
Stairway tomb	-	-	1,9
Bricked grave	76	28,1	42
Rect. shaft	24	8,9	19
Round shaft	2	0,7	1,5
Irreg. shaft	2	0,7	1,7
Lateral niche	6	2,2	1,8
Sand burial	159	58,9	20
Surface burial	1	0,4	0,7

Fig. 31: Distribution of the unplundered, but empty tombs

Here we can see that sand burials especially were interred without objects. There are a number of possibilities why this is so. Maybe there is a chronological aspect to consider – sand burials can be much later in date, since they are often on a higher level than the other tombs. Maybe it has to be interpreted socially: perhaps here we can see the burials of the poorest section of society. Or maybe these people are part of another cultural tradition, which is otherwise not reflected in the burial customs of the sand burials.

II.4.3. Finds which were not found at Sanam

In other Napatan cemeteries types of funerary goods were documented which are not found at Sanam. This may be due to various reasons:

1. The finds were not conserved. No objects of wood or any other organic material are documented.
2. Finds were robbed – objects made from precious materials were especially likely to have been looted. From the few undisturbed graves that were found we know that objects of silver and even gold were used.
3. Some finds are not usual in this social class, like ushabtis or canopic jars, which are restricted to the royal burials. These objects have a connotation linked to the royal sphere and are never used in the segment of the society buried at Sanam.
4. Several finds are not found at Sanam, but in other non-royal Napatan cemeteries, like the bed burial.

II.4.4. Incense burner and offering tables *(fig. 32, colour plate 1)*

From the cemetery of Sanam 17 pottery incense burners and 57 offering tables were found (40 of stone, 14 of pottery, the material for the remaining 3 is not documented). Both object categories are used for funerary rituals in Egypt, but we do not know how they were integrated in the Napatan culture.

The incense burners are shallow or deep cups with a high stand. In one instance, the incense burner is decorated with impressed dots which form rhomboid and triangular patterns.

The offering tables are decorated with *hes*-vases and bread loaves, and very seldom also flowers and vegetables. Some offering tables of stone are combined with deep basins; these may be attached to the side with the spout or at the opposite side. Two more flat pans of pottery were found, which may also have been used for offerings.

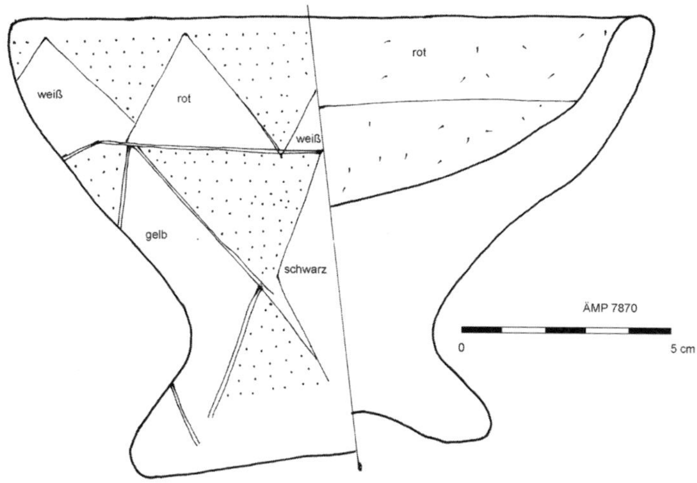

Fig. 32: Incense burner in the Egyptian Museum, Berlin (inv.-no. 7870, drawing: Lohwasser)

It is very explicit that incense burners and offering tables were found mainly in cave graves and stairway tombs (fig. 33).

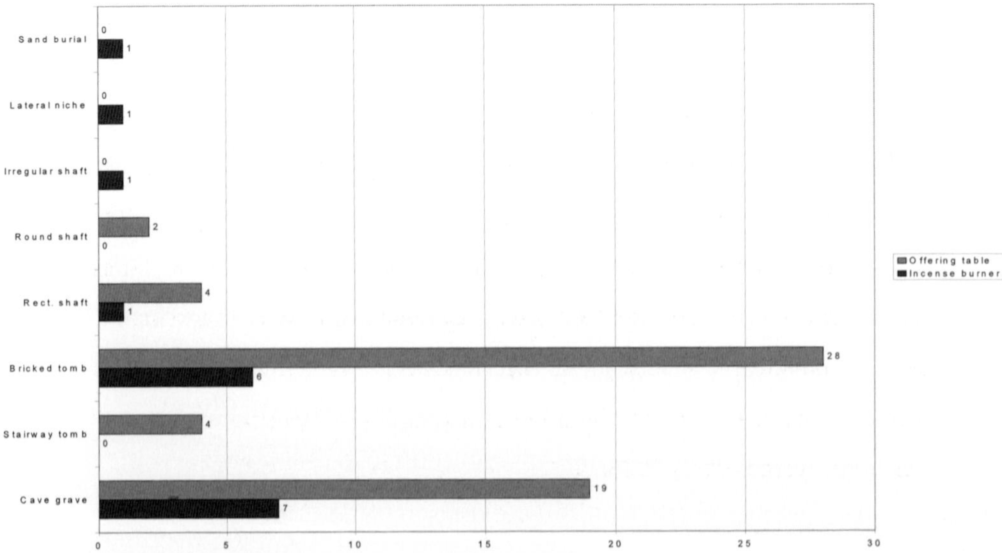

Fig. 33: Presence of offering tables/incense burners according to grave types

Most of the burners and offering tables were found in the debris of the graves, but seven offering tables were found at the lower end of the staircase of cave graves. Two were found outside the grave together with an incense burner, and it seems that this was the primary position. In the royal tombs at Nuri the offering table was positioned in the chapel where the funerary cult took place.[12] All other positions are possibly secondary. It is noteworthy that in several tombs more than one offering table was found:

0007, 0050, 0091, 0135, 0379, 0398: two of stone, 0652: two of burnt bricks, 0046, 1139: three of stone, 0208: five of stone and one of pottery, 0690, 1369: one of stone and one of pottery.

[12] For example in Nu. 20: Dunham 1955: pl. VIII.A, B.

Several offering tables were found in other Napatan cemeteries. Some from the royal cemetery of Nuri as well as one from Meroe are inscribed with offering formulae.[13] The other offering tables from Meroe, and those from Missiminia, Sedeinga and two others from Nuri are not inscribed.[14] Incense burners are not easy to identify in the Napatan cemeteries, since the form of a goblet may be interpreted as drinking cup. But sometimes there are holes in the cup and thus they may have been used as burners.[15] There is no clear connection in the deposition of offering tables and incense burners. In four tombs at Sanam and only very seldom in other cemeteries were both tools found.

II.4.5. Charcoal and blocks of stone

In 23 tombs Griffith documented charcoal. In only three instances was it found in a bowl. Nevertheless, charcoal found in the debris could have been the remains of funerary rites.

In seven cases Griffith found a block of stone which may have been used to close the entrance of the tomb as well as serving as an offering table.

---

[13] Nu. 36, Nu. 8, Nu. 4, Nu. 12, Nu. 44, Nu. 15 (Dunham 1955 : Fig. 12, 36, 135, 164, 175, 193) ; Beg. S 20 (Dunham 1963: Fig. 221H)

[14] Missiminia: Vila 1980a: Fig. 30.8, 112, 115.2 Meroe: Beg. W 477, Beg. S 69, Beg. S 39 (Dunham 1963: Fig. 51.b, 186.10, 205B, 225B); Nuri: Nu. 40, Nu. 56 (Dunham 1955: Fig. 86, 195). Sedeinga: Berger-El Naggar/ Leclant 2006-2007, 42, fig. 3, 4; Schiff-Giorgini 1966: pl. XXX, XXXIV.

[15] Ku. 13, Ku. 71? (Dunham 1950: Fig. 18b, 34b); Nu. 36, Nu. 3, Nu.6, Nu.47 (Dunham 1955: Fig. 10, 28, 38, 130), Beg. W 496, Beg. W 818, Beg. S 160 (Dunham 1963: Fig. 175.1, Fig. A.23, Fig,. 238H). Perhaps the burner found in the late Meroitic tomb Beg. W 308 is also Napatan? (Dunham 1963: Fig. 107.a). Missiminia: Vila 1980a: Fig. 115.1; Kerma: Bonnet 1999: 6, Fig. 9/1.

II.4.6. Bead net and stucco *(see figs. 4, 10, 52, colour plate 2)*

Griffith distinguished between mummies and extended burials which were not mummified. He considered mummies in extended burials to be those bearing the remains of stucco, suggesting that they were originally covered by cartonnage or bead nets. However, since there is no evidence for Egyptian style mummification – for instance canopic jars and mummy-amulets are absent – I hesitate to explain these instances as mummification.

Fig. 34: Bead-net (grave 1428, Ashmolean Museum 1921.807, photo: Ashmolean Museum)

Some bead nets were found partially intact and in these cases Griffith used wax to preserve them (fig. 34). But in most burials there were masses of loose tubular beads of faience. The intact nets were knotted into rhomboid patterns with green or blue tubular beads, and the matching corners were covered with ring beads in different colours. In very few burials Griffith found a complex pattern which he described in the tomb cards. Mostly this consisted of faces or figures woven in beads and covering the face or breast of the dead. Here are some examples:

0179: southern skeleton: beadwork on breast, black scarab with wings of various colours. Above this is a network over the face.

0182: scarab over breast, various fragments further down. Down middle of legs, narrow strip of white beads, with remains of hieroglyphs in black on white ground.

0473: At neck, remains of collar, inner portion red with green, white, red, and black border (some waxed). On shoulders below, wings of a scarab in red, white, black and green, on middle another design, between legs, apparently hieroglyphs.

1398: network of tubular beads, the knots of single ring beads with designs in bead cloth. On face the beads remaining all black and red as far as the chin were there was network. Collar of red, yellow and blue ring beads in pairs, winged scarab on breast, body black and yellow, wings white and blue and yellow, wings probably of crowned hawk (central part missing), between legs a band of hieroglyphs of which a *hotep* and a *nefer* were clear

Parallels of bead nets can be found in the cemeteries in the North (Missiminia and Kerma) as well as at Meroe (Beg. S and Beg. W) in the South of the Empire. They were used in the royal tombs at El Kurru and Nuri too, but there the beads were of precious stone and the yarns of silver wire. The most famous tomb is Beg. S 85, the burial of the king's wife Mernua, whose body is covered by a bead net with interwoven stripes of silver.[16]

The bead net was used in Egypt from the Third Intermediate Period up to the Greek period.[17] The symbolic meaning of providing protection for the dead was intensified with interwoven symbols of recreation. It can only be assumed that the Kushites knew the meaning of these symbols.

In some graves Griffith documented traces of colour, and sometimes traces of stucco. Thus we have to imagine that some of the dead were covered with a stucco cartonnage and decorated like burials in Egypt. Some examples from Griffith's records:

0248: with considerable remains of stucco from cartonnage?, painted with designs in red, pale blue and black, chiefly in fine lines as on papyrus. In succession, broad usekht collar (with two bands of rosettes and bands of lotus petals etc.). Figure of Nut with outspread wings, Re enthroned, goddess behind and table of offerings before him. Anubis standing faced by another deity? Anubis tending the mummy.

1162: cartonnage mask and part of wig remaining, the face red, the wig chiefly white and blue with some red (see fig. 4).

1502A: remains of cartonnage, face red, wig yellow with purple strips. On breast, figures of deities in yellow, red and orange and blue on a white ground, between legs, stripe with black hieroglyphs on yellow ground.

Parallels are known from Missiminia as well as from Mirgissa and Meroe. Traces of coffins in Kerma and Sai hint to a similar treatment of the dead there.

As already stated by Griffith, bead nets or traces of stucco were found

[16] Dunham 1963: 366–373.

[17] Silvano 1980; Aston 2009: 290-293.

predominantly in cave and stairway graves as well as in the large rectangular bricked graves (fig. 35). In every instance, the burial was extended. For Kerma, Bonnet (1999: 4-5) noted that all burials with bead nets were female, but only four burials with bead nets were found. Since we do not know the sex of any of the burials at Sanam, we cannot draw the same conclusion.

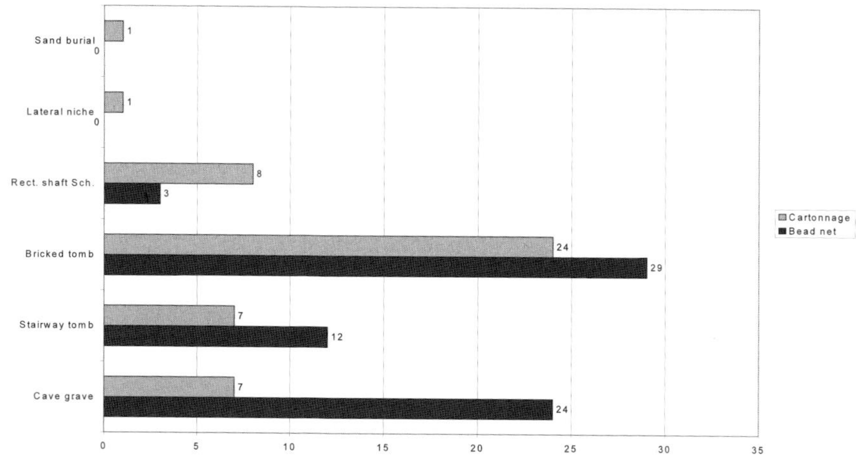

Fig. 35: Presence of beadnet/cartonnage according to grave types

II.4.7. Adornment

Many burials were adorned with different objects which today we class as "adornments". These include diadems, necklaces, earrings, finger rings, wrists and ankle bangles and belly chains. It is difficult to draw a line between decorative adornment and amulets on the body. Even beads of specific materials (lapis lazuli, carnelian etc.) may have had a symbolic meaning because of their colour.

II.4.7.1. Headgear

According to Griffith (1923: 106), no types of headgear were found. However, in tomb 1516 there were the remains of a cap(?) formed by several rows of udjats of blue and yellow faience. Also the 24 udjats in tomb 0698, found at the head, may have been a cap or diadem. In two graves (0714, 1562) several figures of Bes in silver were found around the head, and these too seem to have formed a diadem. Another diadem, a gilded stripe, was found on the forehead again of the burial in 1516. Since several amulets and beads as well as shells were found on the head of some bodies, we can reconstruct them as being an amuletic diadem.

There is no clear pattern in the use of tomb types, but instances of headgear were slightly greater in sand burials.

On the tomb cards, Griffith documented in several graves *coiled beads* or *tubular beads of silver wire.* Since only one is depicted in a photograph, it is difficult to decide if all of them looked the same. There might be parallels in Jebel Moya, where Gerharz (1994: 261) suggested that they were used as adornments of the hair.

II.4.7.2. Earrings *(colour plate 3)*

At Sanam earrings were used in various forms. They can be open rings of metal as well as of faience or stone. Another type is the hollow drop earring that hangs down from the ear. Sometimes these have little holes at the lower end for the attachment of small bells, blossoms or chains. Solid drop earrings made of alabaster, glass and faience were also found. In addition to these were earplugs which resemble little mushrooms or cylinders. In some instances, they cannot be distinguished from lip-plugs.

With some burials only one earring was found, but normally they are documented in pairs. Often more than one pair was found near the head of the burial. In one tomb, 0385, eleven pairs adorned the dead.

II.4.7.3. Lip-plugs

Three plugs in Sanam may have been used as lip-plugs. They are small and look like nails. Large quantities of lip-plugs in different shapes were discovered between the teeth of bodies at Jebel Moya.[18] The examples from Sanam were found near the head but their exact position went unrecorded.

II.4.7.4. Finger rings

Griffith documented 78 finger rings, 26 of bronze, 19 of silver, 2 of gold, and the rest of various stones, shells and faience. The simplest examples are made of bent wire, but rings of cast metal embellished with a signet were also found as well as rings of stone. Some burials contained more than one ring; for example, in 0632 six finger rings adorned the dead. In four instances, the signet bore a good New Year wish inscribed in hieroglyphs.

As with other objects of adornment, finger rings are most frequently found in burials of children and young persons, but they are by no means exclusive to them.

II.4.7.5. Bangles

At least 75 bangles were found, worn at the wrists or ankles and, in most cases, in pairs. 40 are of bronze, 10 of iron, 18 of ivory, one of silver and three of faience. The metal examples are made of a thick wire and the bangles of ivory are plain rings. Only the broad armlets of faience are decorated and these all came from the very well equipped grave 1516 (fig. 36).

---

[18] Addison 1949: LI, LII, LIV; Gerharz 1994: 276.

Fig. 36: Openworked bracelet of faience (grave 1516, Ashmolean Museum 1914.462, photo: Ashmolean Museum)

It is noteworthy that the 75 bangles came from just 21 graves. All the burials with bangles – again mostly of young persons – are adorned with various kinds of jewellery. Moreover, they were wearing more than one bangle, often on the wrists and ankles.

II.4.7.6. Buttons

Two burials were equipped with discs of metal, perhaps originally sewn onto a cloth covering the dead. In 0457 there was a disc of silver found amongst bone fragments and therefore cannot be reconstructed in its original position. In 1516 a row of bronze discs extended from the shoulders to the upper arm on one body. There are also imitations of cowries in faience as well as in metal which may have been buttons sewn on to cloth, since they have sewing holes (colour plate 4).

II.4.7.7. Beads, pendants and necklaces

Beads are documented in nearly all burials with finds, and may have belonged to necklaces. In the following section, I present the different types and materials of beads as well as pendants. As a definition, a bead is pierced through the middle, a pendant on one side to hang down from a string. Amulets, which strictly speaking are also pendants, are presented in the following chapter.

Beads (colour plates 5 – 9)

All the types of beads from Sanam are already known from other Napatan cemeteries. The most prominent forms are barrels, balls, rings and disc beads. Of course, tubular beads might be all that remains of a bead net, but in the instances listed above very few beads were found. Therefore, it is unlikely that these derive from bead nets, although we cannot exclude it. But there are also more elaborated beads, like the double-scarab or eye-beads. Beads which represent blossoms or flowers are present in various forms.

The most prominent material is faience (including paste, which is not distinguishable in the records of Griffith). There are various kinds of stone; most prominent are carnelian, basalt, lapis lazuli, steatite and chalcedony. But also glass and shells were often used. Silver and bronze are the only documented metals. From this table (fig. 37) we can learn that faience was used for nearly all bead types. In particular, the complex forms (flowers, eyes, serrated lentoid) are made only of this material which is easily to mould. Barrel and ball beads were the preferred forms in stone, while discs are made of ostrich shells.

material	ball	barrel	disc	ring	tube	double-tube	cylin-der	lentoid	serrated lentoid	melon	melon keeled	Eye big	eye small	flower	Flower-tube	Crysanth.	Double-scarab	Dumb-bell	facetted	keeled	Rect.	spiral	sum
agate	4	17																					21
alabaster	6	6					3														2		17
amethyst	18	6						2															26
basalt	9	43																			5		57
bronze		3		5	4	4	5															5	26
bronzewire																						5	5
chalzedony	16	22																					38
fayence	103	131	113	248	99		29	3	45	32	2	20	26	24	11	8	2	2	2	3	5		908
feldspar	7	6		3																			16
glass	31	29	5	10	2		13						3	2							3		98
garnet				2																			2
haemathite		2																					2
jasper	9	15					3			4											2		33
calzite	2																						2
carnel	66	74		6			9			3										3	3		164
crystall	2	7																					9
lapislazuli	19	15		3	2														4		3		46
Moss-agate		6																			2		8
shell		6	76	2																			84
onyx		5																					5
ostrich shell			19																				19
paste	23	39	7	23	4		8																104
quartz	6	4					5																15
silver	12	12		5																		3	32
silver, gilded	5																						5
silverwire																						4	4
steatite		10					3			3													16
steatite, burnt		5					2																7
steatite, glased		2										3											5
stone		5																					5
zeolite		10					3																13
sum	338	480	220	307	111	4	83	5	45	42	2	23	29	26	11	8	2	2	6	6	25	17	1792

Fig. 37: Types and materials of beads

Burials with beads are spread all over the cemetery. They are found in all types of graves and their distribution matches the normal distribution. The same is true for the distribution according to the burial pose. Only in the age distribution are there variants: Children and infants are especially well equipped with beads. Another differentiation in the distribution of beads can be seen with (semi)contracted burials on the right or on the left side: Burials on their right side are furnished with many more beads and other adornments. There are also differences in the types of the beads used in the various burial positions: Extended burials were found principally with ball, barrel and flower beads, and (semi)contracted bodies with cylindrical and disc beads.

It is interesting to note that while the main position of beads was around the neck or on the breast, many were also found round the abdomen or at the hips. These beads may have formed girdles and their forms were mainly discs of (ostrich)shells or faience, but also barrel beads. Some of the loose beads were also found at the wrists or anklets.

Beads are also the main find categories in other Napatan cemeteries. They vary in form and material like those at Sanam and occur in private cemeteries as well as in royal tombs.

Pendants (colour plates 10, 11)

The most prominent forms of pendants are drops, stones with holes in the upper end, and poppy pendants. The materials are stones (carnelian as well as pebbles) and faience. There is only one instance for pendants in gold and silver.

The distribution of pendants according to grave types reveals that a slightly larger number were found in shaft tombs and fewer in cave graves. According to the burial pose, many more contracted burials were found with pendants in relation to their presence on this cemetery. And according to the age of the burials we note again that infants, children and young adults were very well equipped with pendants.

Necklaces

In some cases, Griffith recorded the order of the beads and reconstructed their stringing. The following examples are taken from the tomb cards:

0694: Round neck, string of rough carnelian ball beads with shell discs singly or in groups (strung in original order), smallish barrel beads of white zeolite, a lentoid bead of the same. Small barrel bead and ball bead of basalt.

0737: Across waist beneath spine, string of fine beads etc. (restrung in original order) consisting of 6 barrel beads of crystal, 3 of basalt, one of carnelian, plain rectangular plaque of crystal, do. of greenish jasper, plain scarab of crystal, well engraved scarab of burnt steatite.

0879: At lower end of pelvis, a string of beads etc. (strung almost in original order): burnt steatite scarab inscribed Neferkere (Shabako), worn; frog of basalt, white with grey head; rectangular bead of opaque glass, one face convex the other flat; barrel bead, reddish grey speckled (limonite with quartz grains), 2 of basalt, grey and white, one of chalcedony, one of crystal, one of alabaster.

1098: String of black and red paste barrel beads with 2 or 3 shell disc beads at irreg. intervals and a green glaze openwork udjat (strung on spot in almost original order).

1131: Under waist, string of [scarab of burnt steatite] non magnetic haematite scarab "there is no fear", etc., chalzedony ram sphinx, ball bead and flat oblong bead of lapis, ball bead and 2 barrel beads of carnelian, 2 small barrel beads of reddish and white basalt, large barrel bead of moss agate, all strung in original order.

1428: On waist, under beadcloth, string in original order, the large scarab at left side: 5 large barrel beads of carnelian, 2 chalzedony, 2 smaller reddish of basalt, one bluish grey agate, 3 ball beads of amethyst, one of lapis, and half of another, very pale, burnt steatite (Bes between monkeys) white glaze scarab "Amun give life", rect. plaque of bluish glaze.

Examining these strings, one can see that beads and amulets were both included in necklaces (colour plate 12). Maybe the colours or the material had amuletic meaning, perhaps also their form. Apart from normal beads, there were also extraordinary examples with incised designs or painted decoration (mostly of udjats).

II.4.7.8. Amulets

Large numbers of amulets were found at Sanam. Most of them come under the category of seal-amulets, such as scarabs, scaraboids and plaques. These bear short inscriptions or depictions. They will be discussed later. There are many amuletic figures, which have a loop behind the head for attachment. Since in most cases Griffith wrote vague descriptions, for example “string of cats”, we often do not know how many single objects of the same type were used. Therefore, when numbers are given in the following tables, they are not totals of individual objects, but rather every entry of Griffith (fig. 38).

It is easy to see that the most common amulet is the udjat-eye, followed by depictions of gods and goddesses. The udjat-eye is also very common in Egypt during all periods. In Nubia it is greatly used in the Napatan Period, but seldom in the Meroitic Period. The udjat-eyes from Sanam were made of faience, but there are also some of semi-precious stones (lapis lazuli, carnelian, jasper - colour plate 13) and of silver. There are a variety of forms of udjats made from faience. They can be flat and outlined, painted or open-worked (colour plate 14). A special form is the quadruple-udjat which occurs in very detailed as well as crude examples (colour plate 15). Some of the udjats are combined with other elements, like a cat, a claw or a second, smaller udjat-eye (see front cover).

Group	Number
Undetermined figure	3
Object	22
Holy sign	39
Plant	56
Animal	162
God/goddess	307
Udjat	352

Fig. 38: Amulets, grouped according to their categories

Furthermore, amulets in form of various gods were found at Sanam. Most of them are fertility figures like Bes or Pataikos, but Isis (often together with her son Horus) also occurs as well as Khonsu (colour plate 16). The next group are animal amulets. The most prominent type is the frog – made from different materials and sometimes found in large quantities in a single tomb (colour plate 17). Frogs as well as the sow, suckling her piglets, are again amulets which are interpreted as fertility figures. Of plant-shaped amulets, the papyrus is the most common form (see also backpage).

We can conclude that the most often used amulets belong in the spheres of protection and fertility. Their distribution in the cemetery shows a greater number in bricked tombs and fewer in cave tombs. According to the burial positions, there are no differences visible. But according to the age of the dead, there is a clear emphasis on infants, children and young persons.

II.4.7.9. Scarabs, scaraboids and plaques[19] *(fig. 39)*

As with many other cemeteries of the Late Period in Egypt, large numbers of seal-amulets were found at Sanam. These were used as amulets,

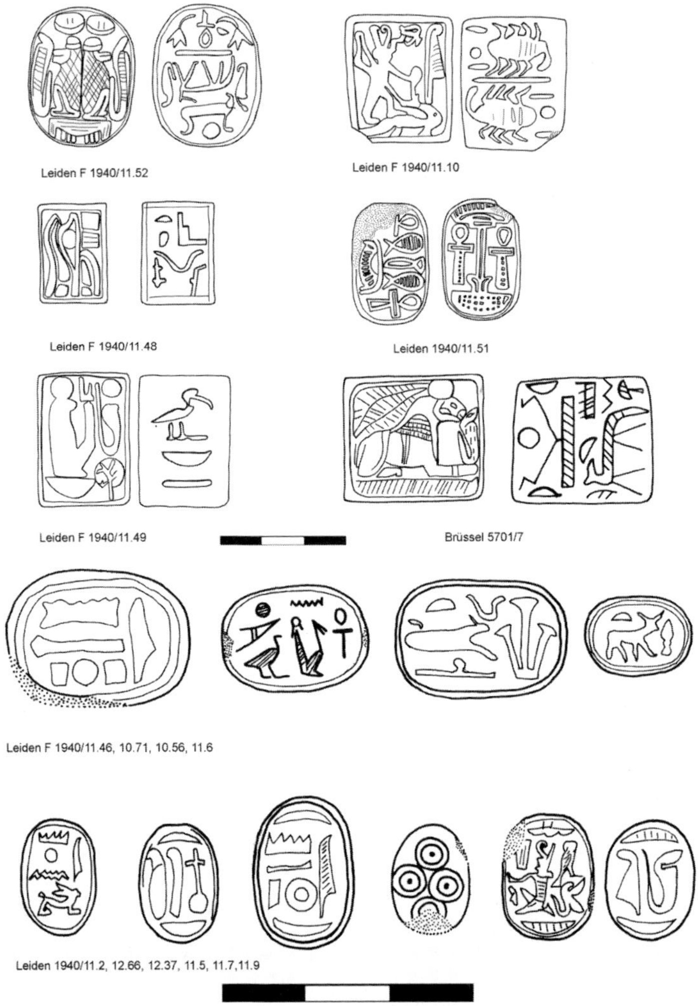

Fig. 39: Some scarabs and plaques (drawings: Lohwasser)

[19] The detailed list with the known locations of objects in museums is presented in the full publication.

but there is no indication that they were also used for sealing. Their amuletic character is present in different ways. First of all, the form itself, the scarab as a symbol of creation, was present in Egyptian tombs throughout many centuries. Secondly, the engraving on the other side very often included symbols of creation, the cryptographic writing of the name of Amun and the depiction or name of a god(dess) or king, all of which are positive and potent symbols. Most of them are decorated in the "Kushite bold style",[20] only very few with fine designs.

Most of the seal-amulets are scarabs (542), but there are also 127 scaraboids, 98 square or oval plaques and 19 cowroids.

It is noteworthy that no heart-scarabs were found at Sanam, although this funerary object was common at El Kurru as well as Nuri.[21]

It is a pity that Griffith very often failed to describe the decoration of a scarab; even on the tomb cards he simply mentions for example "3 scarabs" without any further details. Thus, it is necessary to base the following analysis on the scarabs which are already published in photographs in his report and those described on the tomb cards.

Scarabs with king's names and depictions

Several scarabs were found at Sanam with the names of kings of the Egyptian Old, Middle and New Kingdoms. These were all manufactured posthumously, it was the amuletic function of their names that was desired. But there are also scarabs with names of 25th dynasty kings. Piye,

---

[20] For the terminology see Williams 1990: 16.

[21] It was also common in Third Intermediate Period Egypt (Aston 2009: 384-385).

Shabaqo, Shebitqo and Taharqo are attested, perhaps also Anlamani and Psammetich are mentioned. The name most frequently occurring is Neferkare, the throne name of Shabaqo. Beside the fact that a royal name bears positive power, both the translation "beautiful is the Ka of Re"and the three hieroglyphs have amuletic meaning.

In most cases, the throne name is used on scarabs. It seems that the meaningful translations of these names were appreciated. We know of several throne names of Piye, all of them are present at Sanam. They are written in defective writing and therefore we cannot be sure if it is really his name engraved or if the hieroglyphs are reduced to their symbolic character. However, it is noteworthy that scarabs decorated with the name of Taharqo use his birth name, which has no meaning in Egyptian.

13 scarabs show the figure of a king in action. Like the king's names, his depiction also has positive power.

Other scarabs

There are very few scarabs with private names, all of which seem to come from Egypt. Other scarabs bear names or depictions of deities. The majority mention or depict Amun(Re), the most famous god in the Kushite pantheon. Amun(Re) is also the most popular god's name on scarabs, and his name was very often written in cryptographic script. It is very likely that a number of scarabs which bear three hieroglyphs or symbols are in fact a cryptographic writing of the name of Amun(Re).

There are other scarabs with depictions of animals. The most prominent is the crocodile, which is an evil animal, but also, with its connection to water, is associated with fertility. Fecundity symbols such as the lotus or papyrus plant are also used.

There are various geometrical patterns. These were common in the

Egyptian Middle Kingdom, but were also copied in the Late Period. Sometimes it is difficult to distinguish a Middle Kingdom from a Late Period scarab, but for those found at Sanam we can assume that all are of contemporary manufacture.

A large group of scarabs bear various formulas. These range from the New Year's wish, different positive wishes (good day, all good things...) and some combinations of positive symbols which possibly display cryptographic writing.

Only 29 uninscribed scarabs were found. These mummy-scarabs possessed amuletic powers for the deceased. However, this does not prove that mummification was practised at Sanam!

The upper side

A small number of scarabs do not have the head of a beetle, but that of a falcon, ram or bull. Others have their wings decorated with geometric patterns, as well as uraei, a scarab with wings or udjat-eyes.

Besides the few scarabs mentioned above, some plaques and scaraboids have a decorated upper side. The most prominent motif is the udjat, but also common is the baboon, sometimes two, which are associated with the sun god. Again we find the god Amun, mostly in his representation as Amun of Pnubs, sitting under the Persea tree. Further gods depicted are Hapi, the head of the goddess Hathor and Khonsu.

Other scaraboids bear representations of hedgehog, fish, crocodile, hippo and frogs. All these animals are again symbols of rebirth like the scarab itself. The same is also true for the cowroid, where the upper side is made in the form of a cowrie shell.

Distribution of seal amulets

Seal amulets occur most frequently in bricked tombs with far fewer examples found in sand burials. However, it seems that the distribution pattern of seal amulets was not influenced by burial position or age of the dead.

It is interesting to note that seal amulets were found – assuming they were accurately documented by Griffith – near the hands and arms of the dead. In 75 instances, the seal amulet was found at the elbow. In Egypt it was uncommon to wear a seal amulet at the elbow, but in Nubia we know that several adornments were worn in this position.

Several scarabs were found attached to metal rings, but only three of them were found at the fingers. The others were perhaps strung on a necklace or bracelet.

II.4.7.10. Shells, snails and stones

In several tombs Griffith found shells and snails, as well as stones. Pierced stones that possibly served as pendant are integrated in chapter II.4.7.7, but there are pebbles and natural stones of unusual form which were placed in the tomb intentionally. Both, stones and shells may have functioned as symbols and used in magic.

The most common type of shells is the cowrie (c. *Annulus*), but also *Engina mendicaria*, *Oliva inflata*, conus and *Nerita crassilabrum* were found substantial numbers. Several other types are found only in smaller quantities, such as *Polinices aurantia* or *Nassar gibbosula*, while others occur only in a few cases. Some of the shells originate from the Red Sea, others may even come from the Mediterranean.

The distribution of these objects is similar to that of amulets. They were found mainly in bricked tombs, seldom in cave graves or sand burials, and occur slightly more frequently with extended burials. Again, burials of children, especially infants, are furnished with shells. It is noteworthy that they are buried mainly with cowries, whereas adults had these as well as other types of shells.

Their position on the corpse is different to amulets: shells were rarely found at the neck, more often on the head and at the ankles and hands.

At Sanam not only were shells discovered, but also imitations of shells. These 32 imitations are mostly of faience, but some were of metal. Most were imitation cowries. Again, these symbols were associated especially with the burials of children and young persons.

Griffith recorded 17 convolutes of stones without piercing. Most common were carnelian and chalcedony. According to Griffith (1923: 114), some of them might have served as the raw material for beads or as inlays of now vanished objects.

We know of the deposition of stones also from other Napatan cemeteries and temples as well. Some of them have uncommon forms resembling animals or humans. In the tomb of Queen Chensa (Ku. 4) Reisner found oddly formed pebbles, one of which was covered with gold wire.[22] It seems that these stones were of importance for this royal lady. Near the temple B 700 Reisner found a deposit containing, amongst other items, natural stones.[23] Also in the temple of Soniyat a deposit which included 140 stones was excavated. Zurawski (2005: 296) interprets them as magical objects for a rain ritual, but they may have served as amulets as well.

Griffith interpreted the utilisation of shells and stones as a non-Egyptian custom. But the use of shells and stones in the burial was, as already

---

[22] Kendall 1982: 28-29.

[23] Zurawski 1998: 141.

noted, frequently found in (according to Griffith, 'Egyptianised') brick burials with extended skeletons. It is noteworthy that they also occurred regularly in combination with the remains of stucco (from cartonnage or coffins), but they were never recorded in combination with bead nets. Therefore, we cannot interpret shells and stones as being purely "Nubian" elements in the cemetery at Sanam.[24]

II.4.8. The pottery

In excavations today, pottery is used as the most distinctive artefact for dating contexts and whole sites. Fabric, surface treatment or form can help to identify a chronology. If the original pots or sherds are not available for study, it is necessary to at least have detailed descriptions, photographs and drawings in order to draw conclusions about the material. Up to now it has been possible for the author to check only the pottery which is stored in the Egyptian Museum Berlin and the Musées Royaux d'Art et d'Histoire, Brussels. Thus, the main sources for the following analyses are the few descriptions given by Griffith. He documented 498 vessels as well as 131 "fragm. of pottery". Griffith arranged the pottery in 15 types with several subtypes.[25] But checking his entries in the tomb cards in comparison with the illustrated types, it is clear that the type sketches rarely represent the vessels of a given type.[26] Griffith himself states that especially types XI and XII are sometimes mixed up.

The local fabrics used are mostly brown and handmade, while the imported Egyptian ware is light and wheel-made. It is referred to as *qulla*-ware, which represents the so called *qena*-ware, a hard and light marl

---

[24] Moreover, shells are also common in poorer burials of this time in Egypt (Aston 2009: 385).
[25] Griffith 1923: 95-103.
[26] Griffith 1923: pl. XVII-XVIII.

variation. Griffith also mentions "red" and "pink" without explaining the fabric. Maybe these vessels consist of a mixture of Nile clay and desert clay (Nubian sandstone with kaoline).[27] The pink fabric includes a higher percentage of desert clay and the red more alluvial clay.

The method of manufacture of the pottery is the same as pottery from other Napatan sites: some vessels are handmade, others are wheel-made. Besides Egyptian imports local vessels were also manufactured by the slow wheel method. Griffith (1923: 102) also mentions two vessels formed in moulds.

Several techniques of surface treatment were employed. Griffith mentions polished, burnished, ribbed, incised/impressed, painted, coated and black topped (colour plate 18). The most common type is a painted red line at the inner and outer side of the mouth of cups and bowls. This is typical for local Napatan pottery (colour plate 19).

In comparing the pottery from Sanam with the published pottery corpora from other Napatan sites, one can detect that the forms vary in the different regions. Since the research on Napatan pottery is yet in its beginnings, we cannot distinguish whether the differences are only regional or are chronological as well. With respect to the hierarchical variations, we can compare our corpus with the pottery from the cemeteries of El Kurru and Nuri, which are close to Sanam. However, except for some single vessels, the corpora differ greatly. Thus, we have to assume that there was a variation of the forms used in royal or private contexts as well. A deeper investigation of the Napatan pottery is only possible by studying the vessels themselves, which was not possible for me up to now.

---

[27] For Napatan wares see Williams 1990: 5-8.

II.4.8.1. Revised Typology

By studying the tomb cards as well as the existing photographs, I have tried to check Griffith's typology. For some types only minor changes were necessary, but other types, especially IX-XIII, had to be rearranged. To distinguish both typologies, I used letters (A-R, X) instead of numbers. The extended lists of vessels will appear in the full publication of this investigation.

II.4.8.2. Distribution

The use of pottery as grave goods is most frequent in cave graves and shaft tombs. Griffith documented more than one vessel particularly in shaft tombs, whereas in most of the other tombs only one pot was found. In some brick graves two vessels were found.

The use of specific vessel types is different in each of the grave types, but it is not possible to distinguish between "Egyptian" and "local" deposits. Perhaps the clearest distribution pattern is the frequency of hand made vessels in shaft tombs and sand burials and an increase of wheel made vessels in brick tombs, stairway tombs and cave graves.

The distribution according to the burial pose shows that pottery is more commonly found in non-extended burials. By looking at the different types a specific use is visible: storage jars without handles (Griffith type I, II) are used with extended burials, those with handles (Griffith type III) are in general, but not exclusively, associated with contracted burials.

Most of the vessels were found in graves with adult burials. Children and youths were provided with less pottery.

II.4.8.3. Find spots of pottery in the tombs

Most of the pottery was found very near the skeleton, although vessels were also placed at the corners of the grave. Some vessels were found inside another pot or used to form the cover of a storage jar. (see colour plate. 23). A few vessels were found outside the tombs and may have served as ritual pottery. It is interesting to note that 7 of the 14 graves with external deposits are situated in a small cluster in the north-western central field. All the graves of this cluster are brick tombs and all the vessels were type C storage jars (Griffith Type III) or type R bowls (Griffith type XIII). None of the ritual vessels were special forms, but normal pot types which were found elsewhere in the tombs.

II.4.8.4. Pots with a hole

In about 10 % the pots were deliberately damaged by drilling a hole in the bottom or the lower part of the vessel. Today we are not sure why the pots were destroyed in this way. Maybe they served as symbolic vessels only, and their secondary use as real vessels was avoided by the damage. However, there are other possible causes.[28]

II.4.9. Non-ceramic vessels

Although most of the vessels found in the cemetery of Sanam are of pottery, there are also bowls of bronze, jugs of alabaster and a few vessels of faience. All three categories hint to the wealth of some tomb owners (fig. 40). Valuable metals and alabaster, which had to be imported, as well as complex decorated faience vessels, were seldom found at Meroe and almost not existent in the north. Only the royal tombs had these kinds of grave goods.

---

[28] See for parallels Seiler 2005: 178-184, French 1986: 160.

Tomb no.	Alabastron (AL)	Bronze vessel (BR)	Faience vessel (FA)
0209		X	X
0231	X	X	
0337	X	X	
0430	X		X
0662	X	X	X
0671	X	X	
0950	X		X
1024	X	X	
1062	X		X

Fig. 40: Combined appearance of non-ceramic vessels

II.4.9.1. Metal vessels

Overall, 37 bronze vessels or parts of them were documented. Griffith described them as bowls, cups, cauldrons and shallow bowls. Aside from the strainers, a small number of objects do not fit in this general typology.[29] Only three bronze vessels were decorated, two with triangles and one with bulls. The latter is an import from the Mediterranean,[30] while the two others might have been produced locally.

It is noteworthy that the spatial distribution presents three clusters of graves with bronze vessels.

The distribution according to grave type very clearly shows that bronze vessels were preferred in shaft tombs; in some cases more than one pot was interred. Since in only a few cases was the age of the dead mentioned, we cannot draw a conclusion. Also the burial pose is seldom mentioned, but here we can detect that contracted burials were more likely to be equipped with bronze vessels.

Looking for parallels, we can mention that very few bronze vessels are

[29] 0337: bronze beaker with expanding mouth and flat circular base, H. 12, D. 11Cm; 0846: bronze beaker, fairly strong, sides nearly vertical, bottom rounded, H. 16.5, D. 13, slightly crushed; 0654B: small bronze cup, straight sides, thin, expanding to rim from flat base, H. 4.7, D. 7; 0830: fragments of shallow bronze cup with shoulder and out-turned rim, H. 5.1, D. 14.5

[30] Lohwasser 2002a.

recorded from the north of the country as well as from the royal tombs at El Kurru and Nuri, but many more are known from the south (the cemeteries of Meroe).

II.4.9.2. Faience vessels

Only 16 vessels of faience were found in the cemetery, most of them are already published by Griffith with a photograph. Since most of these vessels are decorated, they form a highlight of the finds in the cemetery. Very few faience vessels are recorded from the other Napatan cemeteries. And with only a few objects, no reasonable stable statistical investigation is possible.

II.4.9.3. Stone vessels *(colour plates 20, 21)*

All of the 54 stone vessels Griffith recorded in the tomb cards are alabastra (vessels with a narrow body, rounded end and a narrow neck for holding oil or perfume). 51 vessels are made of alabaster with just two of steatite and one of rock crystal.

The typology of Griffith, who defined four types, is useful to describe the alabastra of Sanam.[31] In comparison to the other Napatan cemeteries, we can recognise that only type II has many parallels. Type III and IV lack parallels in the other cemeteries, while type I is only seldom recorded. On the other hand, a cylindrical type with broad lip which is found repeatedly at Nuri is not present at Sanam.

In 17 tombs only one alabastron was found, in 11 graves more than one and up to five. It is noteworthy that in most tombs with more than one example different types were used. Maybe these alabastra constituted sets

---

[31] See the typology for the stone vessels found in Third Intermediate Period Egypt: Aston 2009: 386-387.

with different ingredients. They were always found together as convolutes, thus they may have been in a now decayed wooden case (see fig. 12). In tomb 0210, with the alabastra was an inlay of ivory, a rest of an inlayed wooden box. Most of the alabastra were found in brick graves with extended skeletons of adults.

II.4.10. Toilet articles

Several finds from Sanam, such as mirrors, kohl sticks, etc., are included in the category of toilet articles. Very few tools such as small hooks, small spoons as well as needles and tweezers were recorded by Griffith and are not presented here in detail.

Objects in this category were mostly found in shaft tombs and with non extended burials. They are almost exclusively associated with adults.

Mirrors (colour plate 22)

Griffith recorded 15 mirrors of bronze, most of them in shaft tombs in the southern part of the cemetery (see for example fig. 11). The total number is far too small to make a statistical investigation, but 6 mirrors were found with contracted burials, 4 with extended. Looking for parallels in Napatan cemeteries, they found examples only at Meroe and the royal tombs at El Kurru and Nuri.

Scarification instruments

Griffith documented eight tools (iron and bronze), which he described as razors. In several Napatan cemeteries, and a few other sites, examples of a mysterious type of metal implement were found. This tool is very thin and elongated, with a sharp cutting edge on one side, and a broad opposite side with a hole. In most cases there is a hook or spike attached to the rear end. Since this tool is very different from razors and chisels, but is similar to recent scarification instruments of Africa, I would interpret this metal tool as an ancient scarification instrument.[32]

Vanity tools

Several objects fall under the category of vanity tools, like small cosmetic grinders, galena, kohl sticks, but these are few in number. We can only state that the people of Sanam used these objects.

Cosmetic spoons

The two recorded cosmetic spoons of faience are the most famous finds from the cemetery of Sanam. One resembles a girl with a rectangular tray who is interpreted as a swimming girl (fig. 41). The handle of the other spoon depicts a Libyan man with a bag on his shoulder. Whereas the spoon with the girl is contemporary and very probably made locally, the Libyan man can be dated to the New Kingdom of Egypt.[33] Egyptian type cosmetic spoons are not widespread in the kingdom of Kush. A spoon made from half of a large shell is another variant of a cosmetic spoon and examples of this type were found at Sanam.

---

[32] For a detailed discussion, see Lohwasser forthcoming.

[33] Today in the Ägyptisches Museum und Papyrussammlung, Berlin, inv.-no. 3131; for dating this object into the New Kingdom, see Lohwasser 2007; but see also Bulté 2008: 7.

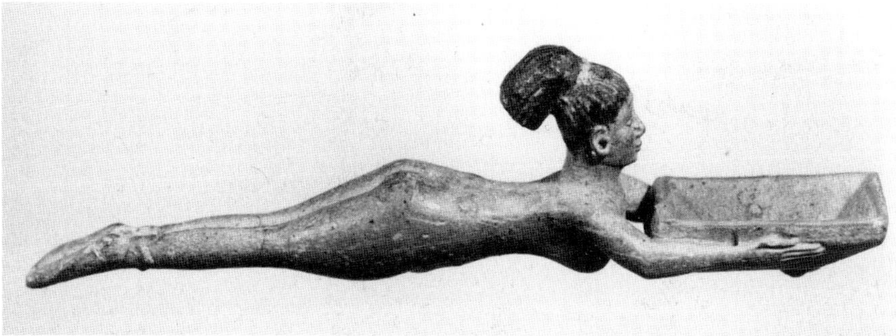

Fig. 41: Cosmetic spoon (grave 0963, Ashmolean Museum 1921.735, photo: Ashmolean Museum)

II.4.11. Imports from the Mediterranean

Looking at the tomb cards as well as the photographs, it is possible to identify several objects that were not made in Kush or Egypt, but were imported from elsewhere. Of those which could be identified all seem to hail from the Mediterranean. It is unclear how these objects came to Sanam, whether they were booty from Egypt or traded luxury goods. However, they were likely to have been items of prestige, since they were only available to a few people.

The most prominent object is a seal of black haematite from Syria. According to Hogarth (1922: 215) it is Hethitic and dates to the late Ramesside Period (20th Dynasty). A flat barrel bead of onyx may also have originated from Syria.

I identified three Phoenician jugs from Sanam in the Egyptian Museum Berlin, but maybe more were found by Griffith (see colour plate 23).[34] His pottery type IV is composed of small jars with only one handle, a type which is unusual in Kush, but very common in the Mediterranean. It is possible that at least some representatives of this type – if not all – had

[34] Lohwasser 2002.

their origin in the Mediterranean.

One of the bronze bowls is decorated with a frieze of bulls. This kind of decoration is typical for Phoenician bull bowls, a group of metal vessels produced for the oriental market of the Assyrian kingdom.

All the imports were found in bricked graves with extended burials, in all but one case with adults.

II.4.12. Various

There are several single objects, which do not belong in any of the already mentioned categories. These are a female figure of burnt steatite, a ball of clay, a few game counters or tokens, three head rests of ivory (of the New Kingdom?), one ostracon with a nearly illegible inscription, four seals (not seal amulets), a few arrow heads, a spear head, two staffs, one nail and a pottery vessel in the form of a cow. All these objects are worth a detailed publication beyond the aim of the present investigation.

III. Perspectives of a cultural-historical approach

In the following I investigate the material from the cemetery of Sanam from several perspectives. The chronological as well as the regional and hierarchical dimensions of the cemetery will be presented. By the end we will discover the level of the individual.

III. 1. The chronology

Griffith (1923: 83) dated the cemetery to the period between the mid-eighth and at the latest the mid-fifth century. Since the use of staircases is not attested before the reign of Piye, he concluded that the earliest tombs, the cave and stairway graves, were constructed at that time. It was Robert Morkot (2000: 138) who mentioned for the first time the possible beginning of this cemetery in the New Kingdom.

III.1.1. The time of use

There are several hints that the cemetery already existed in the New Kingdom.[35] Griffith already mentioned scarabs with New Kingdom royal names.[36] These are Thutmosis IV, Amenhotep III, Ramses II and Sety II. Furthermore, a plaque from the site, which although without a royal name, bears a special style of engraving only attested in the time of Amenhotep II.[37] Thus it might be of that early date. Three ivory headrests, found in graves 44, 963 and 976, might be of New Kingdom manufacture.[38] These are the only headrests found in the cemetery – and the only ones from the presumed Napatan graves. Even in the local royal tombs no such furniture

[35] Lohwasser 2010.

[36] Griffith 1923: 111-112; pl. XLI; XLII.

[37] Griffith 1923: pl. XLVII.13, Jaeger 1982: 222, n. 907 und 248, n. 999.

[38] There is no photo in Griffith's report. The headrest from grave 0963 is visible in fig. 10. The headrest from grave 0976 is today in the Egyptian Museum Berlin, inv.-no. 2960.

was ever found. Given the common presence of headrests in New Kingdom tombs,[39] and the extreme rarity of headrests in Late Period tombs, I think there is a good chance that these headrests maybe of New Kingdom date. Another object probably dating to the New Kingdom is a fragment of a cosmetic spoon. There are parallels dateable to the New Kingdom, which depict exactly this motif.

It is not only objects, but also the tombs themselves that can be dated to the New Kingdom. Although the cave grave with a single axial chamber is very common in Napatan times, no cave tombs with more than one chamber are known except in the royal cemeteries. After a formative phase in the 25th Dynasty, the rule for the layout of royal tombs was: three chambers for a king or ruling queen, two chambers for a queen and one chamber for non-royal persons.[40] Only in New Kingdom cemeteries in Nubia, are there cave graves with several subterranean rooms. A number of graves in these New Kingdom cemeteries were reused in Napatan times. I suspect that this was also the situation at Sanam: the New Kingdom graves were reused several times or were in use continuously from the New Kingdom onwards, until the mid-Napatan period. In sum, we find 39 graves in Sanam's cemetery which were likely to have been already erected in the New Kingdom and were reused in the Napatan period (fig. 42).

We know of some seal amulets, mostly scarabs, with royal names. They contain the names of kings of the 25th Dynasty, as well as Anlamani and probably Psammetich II. All this hints to the Early Napatan and early

[39] See Smith 1992: 205, Tab. 8.

[40] Easily to be recognised in the charts of Dunham (1950: 129).

Fig. 42: Graves and finds of the New Kingdom

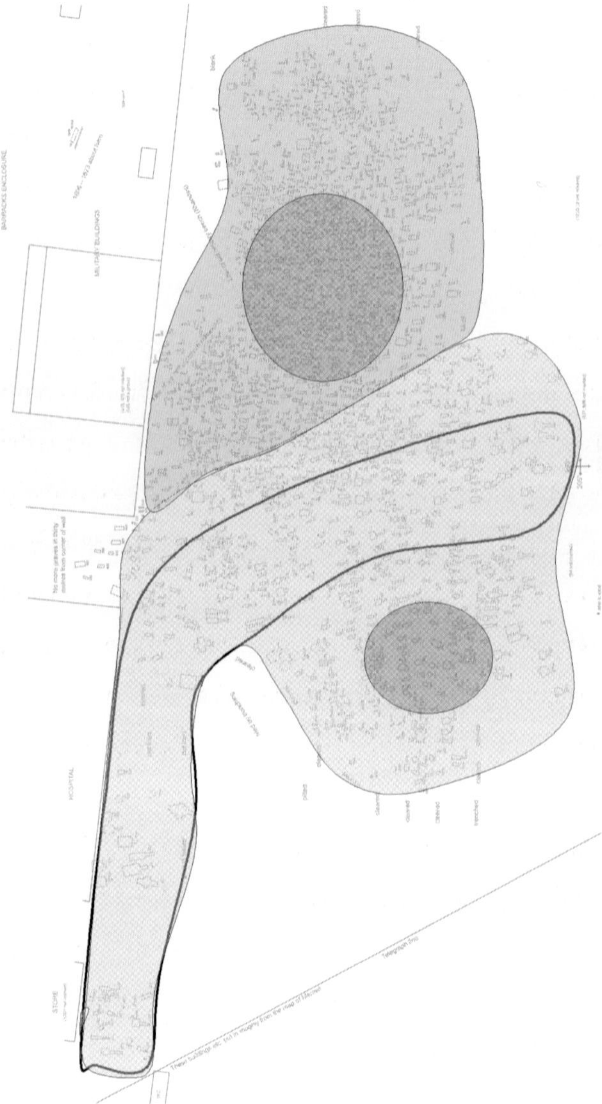

Fig. 43: Evolution of the cemetery in the phase of main use. Black line encircles the proposed outline of the cemetery in New Kingdom, light grey shows the first stage in the Napatan Period, middle grey the enlargement (second stage in the Napatan period), dark grey the consolidation in the third stage.

It is noteworthy that no object with the name of Aspelta was found, the last king who undertook considerable building activity in the temple at Sanam. Even in the recent excavation in the town of Sanam his name has not yet been found.[41] It seems that the cemetery was abandoned before or at the latest in the reign of Aspelta. Also the other small finds as well as the pottery corpus – which, as already mentioned, has not yet been investigated in detail – hint to the use of the cemetery in the first half of the Napatan Period.

It is difficult to establish the development and the internal chronology of the cemetery. It seems that Griffith was right in his assumption that the earliest graves were situated in the south-western edge, where also the tombs of the New Kingdom are identified. The chronologically next group of graves are the stairway tombs, which form a substitute for the cave graves on less stable ground. The shaft tombs and the bricked tombs seem to be the next phase in the development of the cemetery. The sand burials, which are prominent in the northern part, but also spread between shaft tombs in the southern part, albeit on a higher level, are the latest in this cemetery.

It is possible to distinguish three different stages in the development of the cemetery during the Napatan period (fig. 43). At first, the cemetery is reinstalled at the New Kingdom-nucleus in the south-west. These big cave and stairway graves may have housed family crypts. At the same time, small shaft tombs were dug to contain single burials. In the second stage the cemetery was enlarged into the (now) central part. Shaft graves as well as bricked tombs were in use. Maybe the first sand burials were already dug in that stage of the development. The last stage shows the consolidation of the occupancy, especially with sand burials.

[41] Vincentelli 2007.

The three steps merge one into the other and they do not necessarily present the chronological development. It may also be true that three different groups of the population founded three different small cemeteries which grew together over time. It may also be the case that the sand burials represent the lower class population who built their tombs near those of their masters. In this reconstruction, at least the last stage is chronologically parallel to both of the other two stages.

After use of the cemetery ended in the Middle Napatan Period, a small number of graves show secondary use in Meroitic Period. The cave graves 0618, 1200, 1203, 1210 and 1215 contained some Meroitic pottery. Maybe superstructures or even the grave entrances were visible at that time.

We can conclude that the cemetery of Sanam was installed already in the New Kingdom. The main phase of use dates to the Napatan Period, with a few graves reused in the Meroitic period.

III.1.2. The layout of occupation

Cemeteries at important places in Nubia were normally in use for a long time. If we compare the Napatan cemeteries at Qustul, Missiminia, Sai, Kerma or Meroe with Sanam, it is easy to recognise that all of them were used over a very long time span, at least from the New Kingdom to the Meroitic period or even the Middle Ages (fig. 44). In some cases, such as Missiminia, the same cemetery was in use for all the time, in other places, such as Kerma, the position of the cemetery varies in the area. At Sanam, there seems to be another situation. A small cemetery is founded in the New Kingdom, it was enlarged very much in the Early Napatan Period. After about 150 years the cemetery was suddenly abandoned. Only a few traces of Meroitic reuse were discovered by Griffith. Up to now, we lack of Meroitic and Post-Meroitic tombs.

It seems strange that a Meroitic cemetery was not found by Griffith or the local authorities, unless it was already covered by the modern town. At the moment we can only say that at Sanam we find the exceptional situation of a huge Napatan cemetery with only a small forerunner and virtually no subsequent use.

III.1.3. The chronological context at Sanam

Looking at the other already discovered structures at Sanam, we notice that these also date to the first half of the Napatan Period.

	Missiminia	Qustul	Beg. W	Sedeinga
New Kingdom		91		
Napatan	140	32	376	50
Meroitic	377	More than 600	188	severals 100s
Postmeroitic	351	350		2 and secondary burials
Middle Ages	685			

Fig. 44: Comparison of the occupational structure of four cemeteries

III.1.3.1. The temple (fig. 45)

The temple for Amun, bull of Nubia, was founded by Taharqo. It is possible that there was already a temple or at least a shrine dating to the New Kingdom, since Griffith (1922: 85) discovered fragments of earlier statues and even a wall which could date to the New Kingdom. Apart from Taharqo, the names of Tanwetamani, Senkamanisken and Anlamani are mentioned. The last substantial change, a shrine in the hypostyle hall, dates to the reign of king Aspelta. A part of a cartouche of king Malewiebamani (mid-fifth cent. BC) hints to the presence of this king, who is also known from a granite altar in temple B 800 at Jebel Barkal.

Near the temple wall Griffith found some models and unfinished as well as finished objects of faience. He concluded that after the end of its sacral life the temple of Sanam functioned as a faience production area.[42]

Only a few sherds as well as one ostracon date to the Meroitic Period, but the temple itself was not restored at that time. Usually there are Meroitic restorations at sites with Napatan temples, such as Jebel Barkal or Dokki Gel.

Fig. 45: The first court and the remains of the pylon of the temple of Sanam (photo: Fitzenreiter)

There also exist two inscriptions which inform us about the importance of the temple in the time of Anlamani and Aspelta. The stela Kawa VIII mentions the appointment of four daughters of king Anlamani as priestesses in four Amun temples, one of which is the temple of Amun,

[42] Griffith 1923: 88-89, pl. XVII, XVIII.

bull of Nubia.[43] The Adoption stela, dated to the third year of Aspelta, records the succession in the office of the priestess.[44] Again, a daughter of the reigning king was installed as priestess of Amun at Sanam.

According to the archaeological and inscriptional evidence, the temple was in use at the same time as the cemetery: In the New Kingdom and in the Napatan Period up to the reign of Aspelta.

III.1.3.2. The treasury

Griffith (1922: 116-124) excavated part of a building which he called the treasury. It was used for the storage of raw materials (elephant tusks for example), but also a quantity of small finds of metal and faience were found. Some of the finds bore royal names including Piye, Shabaqo, Atlanersa, Senkamanisken and Aspelta.

The excavation of the treasury was completed a few years ago by Irene Vincentelli (2007: 12-14). Therefore, we now know the ground plan: A long building 267m in length, divided into 35 chambers which were used as storage rooms. Again, Vincentelli found small finds with royal names, none of which were later than Aspelta. From the dimensions and layout of the building it is clear that it was a royal stockroom where various goods were collected and stored.

III.1.3.3. The town

During his stay at Sanam, Griffith excavated only a small part of the city near the treasury. This excavation is now continued by Irene Vincentelli.[45] It seems that it was a big town with several large buildings. One of it is called "palace of Senkamanisken", another "palace of the Vizier". Apart

[43] Macadam 1949: 44–50, pl. 15–16
[44] Schäfer 1895, 103-104.
[45] Vincentelli 2004, 2007. 2006-2007.

from a large amount of sealings with the name Senkamanisken, Vincentelli also found an area with many tiny fragments of ivory and valuable stones. This area is interpreted as a production area, perhaps where the grave goods for the royal cemetery were manufactured.

III.1.4. Summary

The time-span which is represented in the cemetery is reflected by the temple, the treasury and the town of Sanam. We can assume that at least the cemetery and temple were founded in the New Kingdom and were revived in the Napatan period. We do not have an early dating for the town up to now, but it is possible that it was founded in the New Kingdom as well. For all the different parts of the site of Sanam, Late Napatan or Meroitic material is lacking.

Given the short period of usage of the cemetery, we can exclude that it was the graveyard of a long-lasting village. We should expect a close connection between the cemetery, temple and the town of the Napatan period.

III.2. Spatial analysis: regional and local specifics

The kings of Kush ruled over a very inhomogeneous territory. The landscape is not formed by the River Nile alone, but also by the different rocks which create various formations. In particular, the appearance of soft Nubian sandstone and hard basement complex has a formative character. Moreover, the Kingdom of Kush is spread over two different climatic zones. In the north there is very dry desert, in the southern part of the empire there is seasonal rain in the semi-arid zone. Further to the south, the rain allows for a savanna zone. These different climatic zones create three distinct types of landscape which were exploited by the inhabitants in different ways. Near the Nile and in the south, permanent settlement with agriculture was possible. Away from the Nile, at least seasonal herding was the subsistence of the people. And in the arid area, only few inhabitants survived with adapted economies.

III.2.1. Regional Differences

Through archaeology, we can at least appreciate the different assemblages of material culture made by these inhabitants. We are aware that these assemblages vary in both their chronological as well as regional spans. In the following, I want to focus on the Napatan Period only, but visit other remains of this cultural phase in different areas (fig. 46).

Location	Napatan Occupation	Notes
Shellal[46]	5 graves in two cemeteries	
Kuban[47]	3 graves	
Qurta[48]	14 graves in five cemeteries	
Maharraqa[49]	4 graves	
Afya[50]	? graves	really Napatan?
Qatta[51]	4 graves	
Aniba[52]	5 graves	
Toshka[53]	1 grave	
Masmas[54]	1 grave	
Qustul [55]	32 graves in eight cemeteries	
Faras[56]	? graves in seven cemeteries	really Napatan?

[46] Williams 1990: 37
[47] Williams 1990: 37
[48] Williams 1990: 38
[49] Williams 1990: 38
[50] Williams 1990: 38
[51] Williams 1990: 38
[52] Williams 1990: 38
[53] Williams 1990: 38
[54] Williams 1990: 38
[55] Williams 1990
[56] Williams 1990: 38

Serra-West[57]	3+x graves in three cemeteries	
Serra-East[58]	7 graves	
Debeira[59]	2 graves	
Debeira 176[60]	105 graves	
Sahaba[61]	3+x graves	
Argin[62]	? graves in 4+x cemeteries	really Napatan?
Gezira Dabarosa[63]	10 graves	
Buhen[64]	2 graves	
Gammai[65]	8 graves in two cemeteries	
Matuga[66]	1 grave with 38 burials	really Napatan?
Mirgissa[67]	27 graves	
Kagarnarti[68]	250 graves	really Napatan?
Semna[69]	6 graves	
Firka[70]	1 grave	
Ginis-East[71]	19 graves in three cemeteries	4 excavated by Vila
Ginis-West[72]	6 graves in two cemeteries	2 excavated by Vila
Attab-East[73]	3 graves	
Attab-West[74]	10+x graves	
Amara-East[75]	39 graves in three cemeteries	Only some excavated
Amara-West[76]	30 graves + 3 more graves	3 excavaed by Fairman, 2 excavated by Vila

[57] Williams 1990: 38
[58] Williams 1993: 133-142
[59] Williams 1990: 39
[60] Saeve-Söderbergh 1989: 200-205
[61] Williams 1990: 39
[62] Williams 1990: 39
[63] Williams 1990: 39
[64] Williams 1990: 39
[65] Williams 1990: 39
[66] Williams 1990: 39
[67] Geus 1975
[68] Williams 1990: 39
[69] Williams 1990: 39
[70] Williams 1990: 39
[71] Williams 1990: 39
[72] Williams 1990: 40
[73] Williams 1990: 40
[74] Williams 1990: 40
[75] Williams 1990: 40
[76] Spencer 2002

Missiminia[77]	140 graves	
Sai[78]	10+x graves	
Sedeinga[79]	Ca. 50 graves	
Hamid[80]	ca. 105 graves in three cemeteries	10 excavated
Hannak[81]	cemetery?	Some Napatan surface finds
Tombos[82]	cemetery	
Soleb[83]	? secondary used graves	
Tabo[84]	cemetery	
Kerma[85]	cemetery	
Kawa[86]	cemetery	some Napatan graves
Hillat El Arab[87]	19 graves	
Sanam[88]	ca. 1700 graves	
Merawi1	1 grave	Excavated by the local people, one Napatan pot.
Gebel Barkal[89]	cemetery?	
Et-Tereif, Site 4-F-71[90]	Kushite Pyramid	
4th Cataract[91]	some graves	
Meroe-West[92]	131? graves	
Meroe-South[93]	96? graves	
Kadada[94]	34 graves in two cemeteries	Few excavated
Sarurab[95]	graves	Maybe datable into the Napatan period

77 Vila 1980a
78 Geus/Lecointe/Maureille 1995
79 Janot e.a. 1997
80 Williams 1990: 40
81 Smith 2003: 89
82 Smith 2003: 138, Smith 2006-2007
83 Williams 1990: 40
84 Bonnet 1999: 3
85 Bonnet 1999: 3-7
86 Welsby 2001: 592-597, Welsby 2002: 36-37
87 Vincentelli 2006
88 Griffith 1923
89 Berenguer 2004
90 Welsby 2004
91 Budka 2007; Näser 2006: 91
92 Dunham 1963
93 Dunham 1963
94 Geus 1984: 35, 75.
95 Eisa 1999: 27

Bauda[96]	graves	Maybe datable into the Napatan period
Gebel Moya[97]	At least 191 graves	
Getaina (White Nile)[98]	cemetery (not excavated)	Some Napatan surface finds
Kawa (White Nile)[99]	cemetery (not excavated)	Some Napatan surface finds

Fig. 46: Composition of Napatan cemeteries and graves

Lower Nubia

This region is located between the 1st and the 2nd cataract. Both are natural barriers which facilitate the emergence of several distinct cultures. Here the cemeteries of Qustul, Debeira and Mirgissa are situated. Throughout the region single Napatan burials were also interred in older graves. But mainly due to the chronological difference between all these tombs (Debeira 176 is dated to the Third Intermediate Period, Qustul and Mirgissa to the 25th Dyn.) and the different appearance of the burials we cannot compare the cultural markers. At Mirgissa, the dead are interred in an extended position in coffins without any pottery, while at Qustul some extended bodies were placed on beds and others contracted in oval pits.

Northern Upper Nubia

This region is situated south of Lower Nubia, between the 2nd cataract and the Kerma Basin. There are at least the partly excavated cemeteries of Missiminia, Sai and Sedeinga. All three of them were in use over a long time span, and all three of them show internal differences in the tomb

96 Eisa 1999: 27

97 Gerharz 1994

98 Eisa 1999: 75

99 Eisa 1999: 75

architecture. Simple pits and bricked tombs have been identified. The burial customs and grave goods seem to be similar in all three cemeteries. In contrast to Lower Nubia, the region of northern Upper Nubia can be called a homogenous area according to the Napatan burials.

Kerma Basin

The cemeteries of Tombos, Tabo and Kerma are situated south of the 3rd cataract. In Tombos and Kerma contracted as well as extended burials were found. Contracted bodies were interred in shafts, extended in coffins in elaborate graves. The excavations in these cemeteries are ongoing and there are as yet no final results published, but it seems that again the Napatan burial customs in this region are very homogenous.

Jebel Barkal

The area around Jebel Barkal is defined by the Holy Mountain which is surrounded by temples. Situated in this region are the royal cemeteries at El Kurru, Nuri and Jebel Barkal. The only non-royal cemetery ground discovered so far is the cemetery of Sanam. Therefore it is difficult to draw a conclusion about the regional coherence according to Napatan burial customs.

4th cataract region

In the first years of the 21st century, many salvage surveys and excavations were conducted around the 4th cataract. The region is flooded today because of the construction of the Merowe Dam. Napatan burials are scarce, but at least some of them could be identified because of the pottery. But the type of graves has parallels only with single graves in Lower Nubia: these are the so-called cleft burials or hidden tombs, which were built between natural rocks, with the skeleton lying on the surface of the stones.

Meroe

In the area of the ancient city of Meroe are two large cemeteries, Beg. S and Beg. W, both of which contain non-royal Napatan tombs. They are very close to each other, but they show different practices in tomb architecture, burial customs and grave goods. The tombs in the South-cemetery are very often marked with pyramids, but there are also some shaft tombs. In the West-cemetery, shaft tombs are the dominant grave type, although in the Late Napatan Period cave graves were also constructed. The grave goods found in both of the cemeteries can be compared with the finds from Sanam.

Gezira

The huge cemetery of Jebel Moya is situated between the two Niles. Moreover, several single tombs were identified in the Gezira region, but most of them are not yet published and are known only from preliminary reports. Therefore, only the cemetery of Jebel Moya is a reliable source for comparison. There are significant differences in funerary equipment: some skeletons show tooth-extraction and many lip-plugs were found. However, other grave goods are similar to the finds in the northern regions, like beads, amulets, metal objects and even some pottery.

III.2.2. Regional embedding

Apart from Lower Nubia, all regions seem to be archaeologically homogenous. The pattern of activity visible in the archaeology is more or less the same in every region: a centre with one or more temples and habitation sites and cemeteries. All major centres are situated at the crossroads of the empire's main routes. Kerma and Kawa are located at the end points of the Maheila-road from Jebel Barkal to the Nile, the Jebel Barkal (or Napata) at the crossing of the Bayuda road, the Maheila road and the Nile, and Meroe at the end point of the Bayuda road (fig. 47).

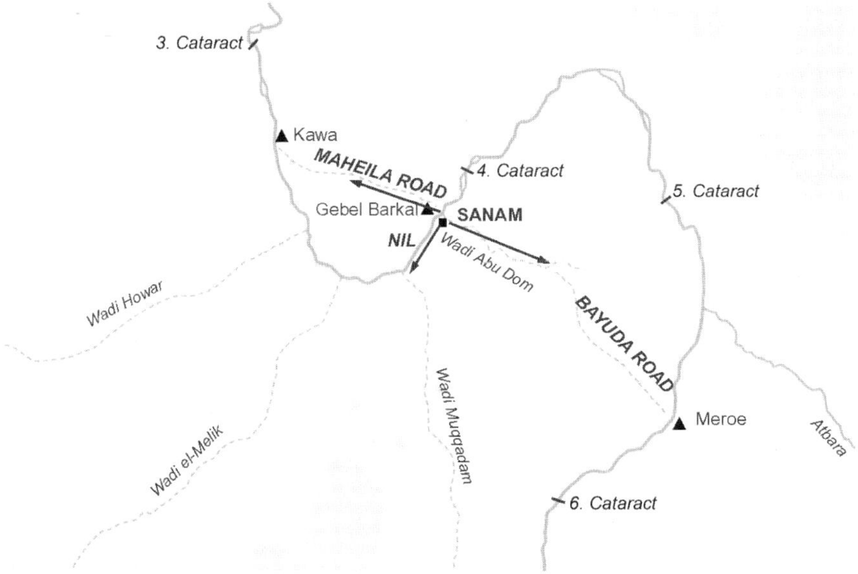

Fig. 47: Trading routes around Sanam

Sanam, situated near the Jebel Barkal at the opposite side of the Nile, is also positioned at the endpoint of the Bayuda road. This route starts near Sanam to the east in the Wadi Abu Dom and crosses the Bayuda to Meroe. North of Sanam the road meets the Nile, maybe here there was the possibility to cross the river to reach Jebel Barkal.[100]

[100] About 4 km north of Sanam, in the village of Qubbet el-Hajj, the new mosque is erected on Napatan sandstone blocks. It seems that there was a temple of that time and maybe it was here that there was a ferry to Jebel Barkal. For this

Already Griffith identified structures within the town at Sanam. These were excavated a few years ago by Irene Vincentelli, who also finished Griffith's excavation of the treasury. The size of the buildings identified so far, as well as the enormous scale of the treasury, indicate that Sanam was a royal town in the first half of the Napatan Period. The interpretation of the treasury as a multi-regional royal store serving as a depot for the collection and storage of trade goods from the north as well as the south is very convincing. A photo of Griffith showing a pile of elephant tusks in one room and the finds of various exotic materials by Vincentelli underline the function of this building for long distance trade (fig. 48).

Fig. 48: Elephant tusks in room 15 of the „treasury of Sanam (Griffith 1923: pl. LIII.b)

---

information as well as for facilitating my visit to this mosque I am indebted to Faiz Hassan Osman and Dr. Tim Kendall.

Many different materials were found in the tombs at Sanam, which do not hail from the region. Stones like alabaster, porphyry, amethyst, carnelian, lapis lazuli and obsidian were imported from other areas. Since long distance trade, especially in luxurious raw materials, was a royal monopoly, it seems that these materials were originally stored in the treasury. The same may be true for the few items of gold and silver. How these precious commodities came to be included in the burials of the citizens of Sanam can only be speculated.

III.2.3. Microtopography

Let us now look at the topographical situation of the cemetery itself. The south-western part and the southern central part are situated in the hardened sand, called by Griffith 'gebel', the graves of the northern central part and the north are on sandy ground. The 'gebel' is hard enough to accommodate cave and shaft tombs, whereas in the sand it was necessary to build bricked tombs.

It is noteworthy that, although in other cemeteries nearby (for example Hillat el Arab or Nuri) supporting pillars were used in the construction of chambers, this was not found at Sanam. Therefore the cave graves are either very small or have collapsed – maybe already in ancient times. Up to now, stairway tombs are known only from Sanam. These stairway tombs are situated in the same area as the cave graves – in the less stable 'gebel'. Maybe they served as substitute cave graves: The shaft tomb was lined with bricks and covered with a bricked vault, therefore it could not so easily collapse. But in order to make a cave and not a shaft tomb, an access by a stairway from the east was needed. In formal aspects, the stairway tomb replaces the cave grave, and provides more stability. Their multiple re-use also resembles the 'family crypts' of the cave graves.

Another special feature also seems to have been motivated by the character of the soil at Sanam. Although the lateral niche grave was very common in the north of the empire,[101] very few were found at Sanam. Again, it is possible that because of the 'gebel's' instability, the niches soon collapsed and so this type of grave fell out of use.

The construction of the bricked stairway tombs and the rare usage of the lateral niche type are typical for Sanam's cemetery and reflect an adaptation to the micrototopography of the site.

III.2.4. Summary

The cemetery of Sanam is situated at the crossing of important roads through the kingdom. The treasury with its finds of stored luxurious materials can be interpreted as royal magazine for collecting trade goods coming from the south or north. It is possible that some inhabitants of Sanam were able to have items made of these materials, since various non-local stones, shells and metals were found in the tombs.

Apart from the regional embedding at Sanam, the local microtopography also played an important role in the setting of the cemetery. Influenced by the unstable ground in which it developed, a type of brick-built stairway tomb was invented and the usual Napatan type of the lateral niche tomb was less common.

III.3. Hierarchical analysis: royal, elite and commoners burials

The cemetery at Sanam is a non-royal cemetery, but it is not the necropolis serving the rural inhabitants who lived for centuries in this area. By combining the data from the town, the temple and the treasury,

---

[101] Lateral niches: Qustul: 32%, Missiminia: 35%, plus 18.5% of lateral niches with trenches.

one can interpret the funerary community as the inhabitants of the city of Sanam. It seems that its heyday lasted for only about 150 years and the burials were made during that time.

The following section seeks to integrate the community of Sanam into the general society of the Kingdom of Kush. Therefore the different social elements – royal, elite, higher and lower status as well as the underclass – are identified.

III.3.1. The place of the cemetery of Sanam in Napatan funerary culture

We learn from this table (fig. 49) that some elements were used only by specific social classes. There are divisions between the tombs and equipment of kings, queens, elite and lower classes. An elite-marker is for example the use of script, which is commonly associated with royal burials (stelae, offering tables, ushabtis etc.), but was seldom used in Beg. S (except for a few ushabtis). Other features such as the typical Napatan pot with red stripe is not present in royal or elite burials, but is common to all the other cemeteries.

From the range of features found at Sanam we can classify the cemetery between the elite and lower class cemeteries of Missiminia, Qustul etc. Some elements which are present at Sanam were also found in the elite cemetery of Beg. S. Other elements which are not present at Beg. S, but occur in other lower class cemeteries, are also found at Sanam. Therefore, the social hierarchy represented in Sanam's cemetery is midway between the elite burials of Beg. S and the lower class burials of Missiminia, Qustul, Sai and Mirgissa. The cemetery of Sanam is more closely comparable with the non-elite, but higher class, cemetery of Beg. W.

Element	**King Ku, Nu**	**Queen Ku, Nu**	**Elite Beg. S**	**Sanam**	**Beg. W**	**Lower class** Missiminia, Qustul, Sai, Mirgissa
3 subterranaean rooms	X	–	–	–	–	–
Funerary stela	X	–	(X)	–	–	–
„water bottle“	X	X rare	–	–	–	–
Foundation deposit	X	X	–	–	–	–
2 subterranaean rooms	(X)	X	–	–	–	–
Decorated room	X	X	–	–	–	–
Heart scarab with inscription	X	X	–	–	–	–
Pyramid	X	X	X	–	–	–
Chapel	X	X	X	–	–	–
Offering table with inscription	X	X	X	–	–	–
Medium „script“	X	X	X	–	–	–
Stone vessel	X	X	X	–	–	–
Mummy amulet	X	X	X	–	–	–
Finger covers	X	X	X 1x	–	–	–
Canopic equipment	X	X	(X)1x	–	–	–
Ushebti	X	X	(X) rare	–	–	–
Djet amulet	X	X	X	–	–	–
Gaming pieces	–	X rare	X	–	X rare	–
Menat amulet	X	X	(X) 1x	(X) 1x	–	–
Decorated bronze vessel	X	X	X	(X) 1x	X rare	–
Box with inlays	X rare	X rare	X frequent	(X) 1x	–	–
Mirror	X	X	X	X	X	–
Kohl-stick	X	X	X	X	(X) 1x	–
Material silver	X	X	X	X	X	–
Material gold	X	X	X	X	X	X rare
Bronze vessel	X	X	X	X	X	(X) 1x
Fayence vessel	X	X	X	X	X	X rare
Alabastra	X	X	X	X	X	X rare
Scarab with recent royal name	–	–	–	X	–	–

Armlet ivory	–	–	–	X	X	–
draughtsman	–	–	–	X	X	X rare
Earring	X rare	X rare	–	X	X	X
Armlet metal	X rare	–	–	X	X	X
Shaft	–	X	X	X	X	X
Offering table, no inscription	–	–	X	X	X	X
Stones	–	X rare, early	–	X	(X) 1x	(X) 1x
Scarab Menkheperre	–	–	–	X	X	X
Scarab with inscription	X rare, early	X rare, early	–	X	X	X
Nubian pottery, type Q	–	–	–	X	–	X rare
Nubian pottery, type R	–	–	–	X	X	X
Pilgrim flasks	–	X rare	X rare	X	X	X
Shells	–	X rare	X rare	X	X	X
God(dess) amulet	–	X rare	X	X	X	X
Bes	–	X rare, early	–	X	X	X
Plaques	–	–	(X) 1x	X	X	X
Animal amulet	very rare	rare	X rare	X	X	X

The following elements seem to have no hierarchical connotation:

Ring	X	X	X	X	X	X
Coffin	X	X	X	?	X	X
Cartonnage	X	X	X	X	X	X
Egyptian pottery	X	X	X	X	X	X
Semi-precious stone	X	X	X	X	X	X

Fig. 49: Different characteristics of funerary culture hierarchically arranged

III.3.2. The funerary community at Sanam

We know already that Sanam had its heyday between the reigns of Piye and Aspelta. The production areas in the town imply that grave goods for the royal cemeteries were manufactured there and that there were skilled sculptors for this task at Sanam. The temple would also have needed architects and sculptors, as well as priests for the cult. The palace would have required a range of service providers and, similar to the treasury, administrative employees.

Fig. 50: Adoption stela
(Louvre C 257, assembled after Schäfer 1895: 103-104)

The Adoption stela, dated to the third year of Aspelta, and most probably originally from Sanam, lists eleven officials who fulfilled the order of His Majesty to introduce Henuttakhebit into the office of a singer of Amun (fig. 50).[102] At the end of the inscription a list of fifteen witnesses with titles and names is given. These are the only non-royal names we know of from the Napatan period. The officials are representatives from different parts of the country, but the witnesses seem to all be priests and a scribe from the temple at Sanam. We can assume that the latter were interred in the Sanam's cemetery.

The dead in the cemetery at Sanam represent the inhabitants of a flourishing town: skilled craftsmen, priests and, most probably, administrative personal of the treasury etc. But none of them has left any inscription.

If this cemetery was really the burial ground of the town, we should expect a wide range of different hierarchical levels represented in the grave goods. This is difficult to analyse, since a lot of the graves were plundered. Although only 484 graves were found undisturbed, it is nevertheless possible to detect specific elements which might serve as indicators for the presence of different social levels.

Firstly, luxury items which are not present in the lower level Napatan cemeteries could hint at the higher status of the buried person. These are goods in precious materials like gold and silver and vessels of bronze, alabaster and faience, as well as mirrors. Items of gold or silver were seldom combined with luxury vessels or mirrors. If we look at the distribution of graves with these goods, one can see that they are associated particularly with shaft graves and bricked graves, but only a few sand burials were equipped with them (fig. 51).

---

[102] Schäfer 1895; see also the translation and comments in FHN I: 259-268.

Grave type (GT)	Graves with aabastra, bronze vessels, fayence vesssels, mirror or precious metal	Percent of tombs with these finds (%)	Percent of this type in the whole cemeter y (%)	Percent of this type with finds in the whole cemetery (%)
Cave grave	9	7,9%	10%	11,8%
Bricked tomb	65	57%	42%	45,2%
Rectl. shaft tomb	24	21 %	19%	20,2%
Round shaft tomb	3	2,6%	1,5%	2,1%
Irreg. shaft tomb.	2	1,7%	1,7%	2,6%
Lateral niche	5	4,4 %	1,8%	1,7%
Sand burial	6	5,3%	20%	12,1%

Fig. 51: Distribution of luxury objects and precious metals according to grave type

For this analysis it is necessary to exclude disturbed graves and burials. These are graves where Griffith documented not only plundering or other forms of disturbance, but also multiple burials, since in these cases the interment of a second or third burial could result in the robbing of goods from the first one. Therefore, all cave and stairway graves are excluded, since all of them were multiple burials. More than half of the intact, but empty, graves were sand burials. Intact burials with luxury grave goods are more often associated with rectangular bricked or lateral niche graves. However, besides the grave goods in intact burials, one can find empty tombs, others with few and simple grave goods, and those with large quantities of luxury grave goods. Therefore, we can interpret the funerary community at Sanam as representative of the town: The few (6%) rich equipped tombs belonged to a local elite, the more normal equipped tombs

(38%) reflect the middle class and the large number of empty tombs (56%) were of the lower class. Of course there is a problem with the latter tombs: they can have been equipped with items of organic material which have not survived.[103] But this is assuming here that these people were socially distinct from the wealthy and influential group with the more elaborated grave goods.

III.3.3. Summary

The attributes in the cemetery of Sanam, the architecture of the tombs and the categories of objects found, are comparable to attributes in the cemetery Beg. W. Both represent a middle-class cemetery with elements of the elite as well as some belonging to the underclass. Moreover, there is visible inner hierarchy in the burials at Sanam. There are some well equipped graves and a lot of poor ones, which mirrors the social hierarchy in the town. A local elite and their dependants together with some very poorly equipped inhabitants were buried at Sanam.

III.4. Ethnic and cultural analysis: the problem of acculturation

III.4.1. Ethnicity

The discussion of ethnicity and acculturation has been revived in recent years. At first glance, the cemetery of Sanam with all the different burial practices, grave goods and tomb types forms an adequate sample for the investigation of these topics. Reisner and Dunham found an ethnic interpretation of the different burial practices in the cemeteries of

[103] The really poor of the same time in Egypt were interred without any grave goods, too (Aston 2009: 396). Since the preservation of organic material was much better in Egypt than in Sanam, I want to conclude that the undisturbed and empty graves in Sanam were indeed without objects.

Meroe.[104] Griffith and Vila defined cultural groups.[105] At Sanam and Missiminia traditional Nubian as well as innovative Egyptianised groups are apparent in the population.

Meanwhile, it is generally accepted that ethnicity is a self-defining system: "The most fundamental point is that ethnic communities are not immutable biological or ontological essences, but the results of historical processes, or, as one might put it, historical processes themselves."[106]
There is of course a problem to identify the Nubians by their self-definition. They left only few texts for us, and the major corpus is written in Meroitic which is not understandable as yet. Furthermore, except in the royal sphere, they left hardly any depictions and thus it is impossible for us to draw an accurate picture of Nubians and their self-constructed ethnic boundaries.

III.4.2. Archaeological culture

Another possibility would be to examine the Napatan material culture. But this also seems to be impossible: We can detect regional differences from Lower Nubia down to the few Napatan remains near the 6th cataract, and with the recent fieldwork at the 4th cataract we learn that there are different cultural traits away from the main habitation centres. Apart from all these differences we also have to bear in mind that our comparison of cemeteries is based only on parts of the material culture.

Since the cemetery of Sanam is the largest non-royal cemetery known today, it makes sense to use this database to identify classifications for the archaeological remains of "Napatan funerary culture".

---

[104] Dunham 1963: 1.
[105] Griffith 1923: 88; Vila 1980b: 35-37.
[106] Pohl 1998: 8.

Type of grave

We have already learned that there are different types of graves at Sanam. In my opinion, the choice is motivated by the type of ground ('gebel', sand), the type of burial community (single burial, family crypt) and chronology as well. In comparison with other Napatan cemeteries we find grave types which are not present in the other cemeteries and grave types in other cemeteries which are not present at Sanam. Therefore the category of grave types seems to be an inappropriate cultural marker.

Burial pose

At Sanam, about 80% of the skeletons were extended and 20% (semi-) contracted. At other Napatan cemeteries both burial poses occur also. Griffith interpreted a group of extended skeletons as "mummies" because they were laid in coffins under bead nets or had stucco masks. But in no case was a heart scarab, mummy amulets or canopic jars found – these objects are the minimum equipment for mummies in Egypt. In contemporary graves in Egypt, they are found with middle and upper class burials, but are absent from lower class burials.[107] Apart from the material remains which can hint to mummification, we have to bear in mind that the preservation of the corpse was a central concept in the imagination of the Egyptians. Up to now, we have no hint of this concept in the kingdom of Kush.

Griffith and others have discussed the extended burial poses and (semi-) contracted body position as indicators of the degree of Egyptianisation. All of the authors agree that the individuals are members of the Napatan archaeological culture, but some are traditional ("Nubian") and others are innovative ("Egyptianised"). If we accept that at Sanam one group of the

[107] See the discussion in Aston 2009: 299.

inhabitants were very traditional and strongly connected with the indigenous culture, while another had already become acculturated to the dominant and advanced Egyptian civilisation, this difference should also be visible in the choice of the accompanying grave goods. We have already learned that both burial poses are present in various grave types, but the non-extended body are most common in shaft tombs. If more than one skeleton was interred, the use of a similar burial position was preferred. Thus, extended bodies were accompanied with extended bodies and contracted with contracted.

In the next section we analyse which grave goods are combined with each pose. Some objects are only present with extended burials, namely bead nets, traces of stucco etc. Also, incense burners and offering tables are found combined only with extended burials. Certain other objects or special types of objects are combined only with extended bodies (faience vessels, cowrie imitations, pottery type H) or with contracted burials (stones, braziers), while others are mainly, but not exclusively, associated with contracted bodies (pottery type R, bronze vessels).

It is significant that some types of grave inventory are combined with a specific burial pose, but virtually none are exclusive. It is not possible to distinguish precisely between the associations of objects or to define an invariable pattern.

We have to assume the combination of different types of markers. It is not the permanent combination of single markers but the sometimes intersecting, sometimes singular appearance of distinct phenomena. All we know of the Napatan funerary culture up to now is that there are no constant universal cultural traits.

III.4.3. Acculturation

The term acculturation was introduced into the scientific debate in the late 19th century.[108] Acculturation is the dialogue between cultures, the process of intercultural exchange, which can lead to the change of artefacts, customs and beliefs. Investigations into acculturation should focus only on small time spans – since the results of acculturation can change with the ongoing process of acculturation – and relate to separate for different population groups. At this point we again face the problem of the sources for the Napatan culture: the chronological stages are far from clear and distinctions between separate social groups are even more difficult to determine.

Another problem is differentiating between acculturation and imitation of the elite: in the New Kingdom, the local elite attempted to imitate Egyptians as much as possible, since identification with the ruling culture could have been an individual's strategy to reach higher up in the local hierarchy. It seems to be impossible to detect these different processes in the archaeological record. But we have to bear in mind the analytical difference between acculturation (dialogue between cultures) and imitation of (Egyptian) elite as a strategy.

Another problem should be addressed here, too. Different results of acculturation (acceptance of foreign cultural traits, adaptation of specific traits on different levels, or resistance to them –all with variations between these results) can operate on different levels:

- formal aspect: the form of the object, the material, the technology. The object can be imported from Egypt, or can be a local imitation of an Egyptian prototype. Here we can detect direct absorption or intentional variations.

---

[108] For a discussion of earlier literature, see Gotter 2001.

- Symbolic aspect: the meaning of the object or its decoration. Here, too, the Egyptian meaning can be incorporated in the local culture, but it can also be an Egyptian object with another, local meaning.
- The contextual aspect: the specific utilisation of the object in the specific context. An Egyptian object which maintains its Egyptian meaning can be included in a different local context. On the other hand, an Egyptian object can be charged with a local meaning, but be present in the normal Egyptian context.

There are many possible variations, but I will present only two examples of this investigation here.

The burial customs

The extended pose was imported from Egypt already in the New Kingdom which resulted in its nearly complete adoption. In the Napatan period, some 700 years later, this pose was already integrated into the indigenous Nubian tradition and was, in my opinion, not interpreted as "Egyptian" at that time. Both poses, the (older) contracted and the (younger) extended positions were both integral to the Napatan funerary tradition. The link between the burials of the New Kingdom and Sanam are provided by the extended burials from graves at Hillat el Arab, where all the documented burials are extended.

Again, already imported in the New Kingdom were several items, such as coffins, which were combined with the extended position burials. Other items, including ushabtis or canopic equipment, were present in New Kingdom Nubia, too, but were absent in the Napatan period. This suggests that although some elements of Egyptian burial customs were adopted into Nubian burial practice, the underlying concepts remained Nubian. Here, then, it is possible to speak of Egyptian cultural traits integrated in the Nubian cultural pattern.

Amulets

The forms of the amulets found at Sanam are entirely adopted from Egyptian culture: Egyptian gods, animals and plants in Egyptian style, and Egyptian symbols. Most of the categories of amulets were already present in New Kingdom Nubia; therefore, a long tradition can again be expected mainly for the older forms like the udjat-eye. Other forms, like the quadruple-udjat, were introduced in Egypt in the Third Intermediate Period or Late Period, thus we can exclude Nubian self-creation. It is questionable if, unlike the form, the meaning was also integrated in the local culture. All in all, we have to imagine a protecting and reanimating amuletic force, but it would be useful to investigate the power inherent in every type of amulet – in Egypt and in Nubia. The context in which the amulets from Sanam were used is not as clear as in Egypt. In Third Intermediate Period and Late Period Egypt, amulets protected women and children.[109] Since we do not know the sex of the skeletons, we cannot interpret the use of amulets in this way.

It is noteworthy that, although numerous types of amulets were used in Nubia, there were many – which were common in Late Period Egypt – that were not used at Sanam. Some amulets (such as the *menat* and *djed*) were found in royal contexts, others in the higher elite burials at Beg. S. Still others, such as Bes or animals, were used only in non-elite contexts. At first glance, the choice of the type of amulet is hierarchical. But it may also be true that there existed different concepts about the necessities required by the dead person. In this case we can detect phenomena of acculturation: In the royal classes, Egyptian concepts of amuletic equipment are present, whereas in the non-elite part of the population

[109] Aston 2009: 374.

indigenous ideas were passed on. There only these types of amulets were used which can be integrated into the local concepts.

III.4.4. The appearance of Napatan funerary archaeological culture

The pattern of Napatan material culture as a whole is diverse. In appreciating their funerary culture we face regional, chronological and hierarchical differences. Moreover, there are different stages and different levels of the resultant acculturation, which lead to a very complex picture. There are at least three detectable roots for cultural indicators:[110] Some are old indigenous traits, others are originally Egyptian elements, which were introduced in the New Kingdom to Nubia and were therefore already incorporated in the tradition. And lastly there are infiltrations of recent Egyptian Late Period elements. Of course we have to expect other influences, too. Possible contacts with cultures along the Blue and White Niles, contacts with nomadic groups in the deserts and contact with Arabia via the Red Sea – traces of all these different cultures may also be present in the Napatan archaeological culture. But since none of these other cultures have been investigated enough to identify their elements in Nubia, we can state only that it is necessary to bear them in mind.

At Sanam, the combination of specific grave types with specific burial positions and particular grave goods is by no means clearly delimited. We can detect tendencies, but they overlap with other groups. Some of these groups show phenomena of acculturation. But equally, we have to expect the tendency of the elite to imitate. The specific feature of the Napatan funerary archaeological culture seems to be the possibility that many variations in all levels of (self-)presentation were present.

---

[110] Comparable with the elements of the Meroitic culture as highlighted by Hintze (1979).

III.4.5. Summary

Interpreting ethnicity as a self-defining system, it is impossible to detect "objective" ethnic groups in the complex documentation from Sanam. The investigation of Napatan material culture results in the realisation that we have to appreciate considerable regional differences. Therefore, we have had to reduce our sources again to just the material culture of Sanam itself. Even there, we can detect various influences, some of them caused by the results of acculturation on different levels.

III.5. Analysis of the individual – the presentation of identities

Several factors can influence the appearance of the burial customs at Sanam, namely chronological, regional and topographical, social and cultural. But as the burials were made by humans, we have to deal with the influence of individuals too. Humans do not act "typological correct", therefore we have to expect a mixture of elements of distinct groups.

In recent years there has been much discussion as to who influenced specific burials – the deceased, who dictated the type of burial in advance before his death or the bereaved, who was/were responsible for burying the dead. Since we have no written evidence from Sanam, we cannot detect who made these choices, but we can be sure that whoever it was had influence and that the burial type was not totally predetermined by an overlaying structure.

III.5.1. Habitus and identities

Every society is bound to a certain degree in a specific habitus. Within this social system, the person has freedom to represent elements of his identity, and to hide other parts. Therefore, every human being has the possibility to create and visualise his identity. In archaeology, we are restricted in tracing singular identities, since our sources are reduced to the archaeological remains. We lack the bodily representation of the living, the domestic environment, the knowledge of how they behaved and acted – therefore, the possibility of being able to reconstruct specific identities is very small.

In the first place, I want to detect the habitus of the Napatan funerary society. This means that I will try to trace signs of representation which form specific groups in this archaeological context. The "structuring structure", the overlying pattern which identifies different groups, is generated by the acts of individual people. Variations in this pattern reveal the individual's freedom to act.

All activity is done in a specific context, which is called the "field" in the theory of practice by P. Bourdieu.[111] In our case, we deal only with the field of burial customs. Every group with its own habitus used specific forms of representation. Of course not every activity, even in a funerary context, leaves traces. The grave type, burial position, burial equipment and grave goods, together with the overall composition of every single burial are our sources for habitual and individual actions.

III.5.2. Codes of representation

Every single group – no matter if is the family, social status, age or any other factors influencing the creation of these groups – is distinguishable from another group. Again, the only signs we can detect of this difference is present in the material culture. Thus, we first try to generate more or less clearly delimited groups based on their funerary assemblages. In

[111] Bourdieu 1977.

order to achieve this I used correspondence analysis[112] and detected the following groups:

Burials with bead net and/or cartonnage (fig. 52-54)

It is evident that 79 burials form a distinct group. All of these were covered with a bead net and/or a cartonnage. Even though I assume that these were not (Egyptian) mummies, they were all buried extended and in most cases in bricked tombs. Only a few of them were found in rectangular shafts. Some of the bodies were equipped with amulets, jewellery and a few pieces of pottery, but the kind and quantity differs very much. Only four burials have other categories of grave goods.

Within the group of burials with bead net and/or cartonnage, we can detect three subgroups: the largest (49 burials) have no further objects, a second group (20 burials) was equipped with amulets and/or jewellery, but without pottery. A third group (6 burials) has only pottery in their grave. Only 4 burials were accompanied with both categories (amulets/jewellery *and* pottery). There are four undisturbed burials, two with bead nets, two with cartonnage, which have far more grave goods. All of them are singularly different and therefore cannot be compared, but there is a connecting element between them: They are equipped with luxury items such as alabastra or gold/silver.

Luxury objects are exclusive and therefore have symbolic value. Normally, they are interpreted as evidence for the high status of the buried

[112] I used the program WinBASP (made by I. Scollar, Bonn). I wish to thank S. Seidlmayer for his instruction and help.

Fig. 52: Grave 0976: burial with bead net (photo: Griffith-Institute)

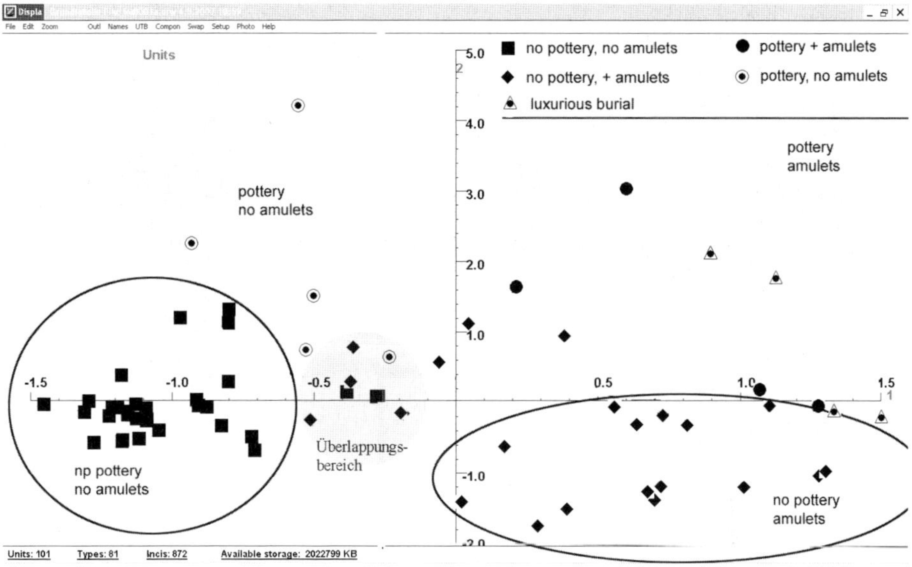

Fig. 53: Correspondence analysis: All burials with bead net/stucco

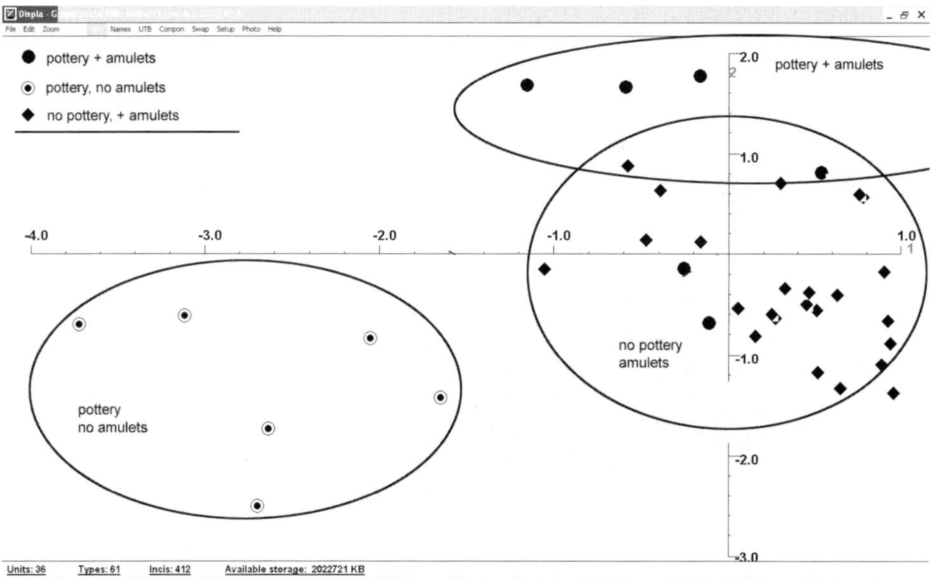

Fig. 54: Correspondence analysis: Burials with bead net and/or stucco and pottery and/or amulets

person. But we have to bear in mind that they may convey messages which we cannot understand because we do not know the system of their codes. These objects did not serve only as grave goods, but also on other communication levels. The codes were known within the boundaries of the group's habitus, but there was enough freedom for individuals to be able to represent their own identity.

Non-extended burials (fig. 6, 7, 8, 11, 55)

Like the previous group, (semi-) contracted burials also form a specific group. This group consists of three subgroups. Again the graves of one subgroup were totally empty. The second subgroup consists of burials with pottery (and sometimes body adornments). The third subgroup was equipped with amulets (and sometimes body adornment). Again, there is a small overlap between subgroup 2 and 3, since a few burials had pottery as well as amulets. And again there were some burials which contained richer or luxury items.

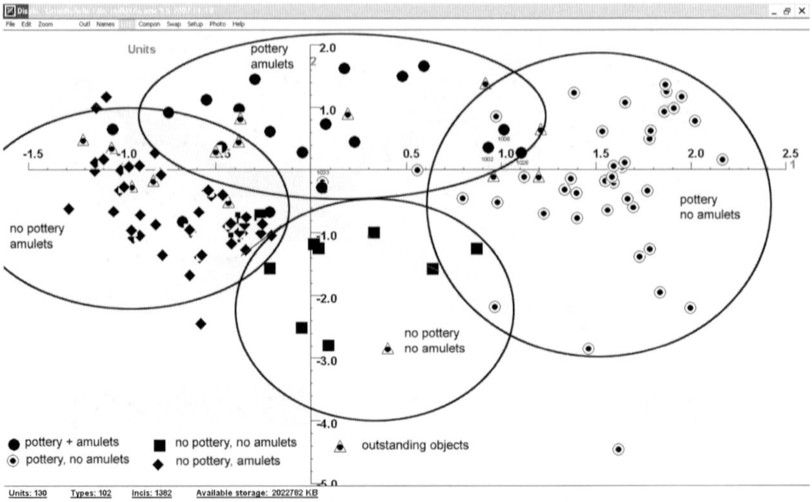

Fig. 55: Correspondence analysis: All non-extended burials

Burials with pottery (figs. 8-11, 56, 57)

Since we can see the same pattern in both groups, specifically those subgroups which are divided by the appearance of pottery, we should investigate as a next step the burials with pottery. We can distinguish four subgroups within the group of burials containing pottery: 1. extended with amulets; 2. extended without amulets; 3. non-extended with amulets; 4. non-extended without amulets. Any overlapping is very limited between these groups, indicating that all the other grave equipment is bound to each specific group. In the technical operation of the correspondence analysis the main factor for the division in the subgroups is the adornment

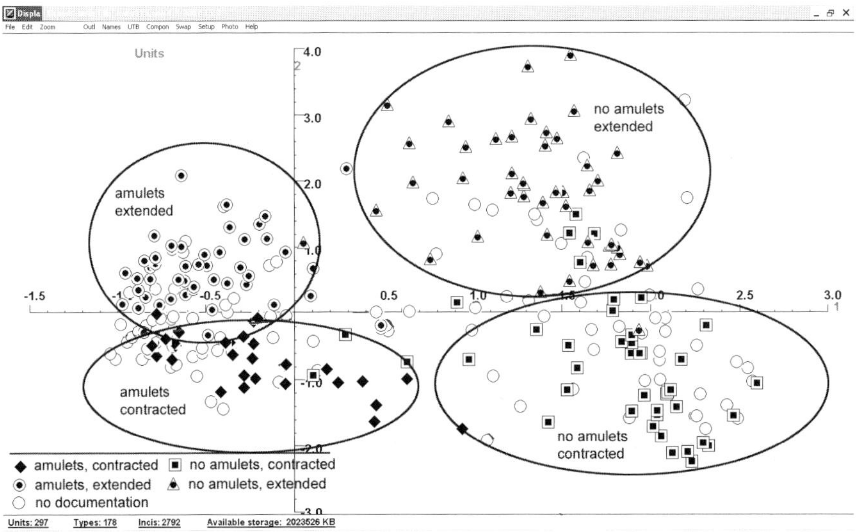

Fig. 56: Correspondence analysis: All burials with pottery

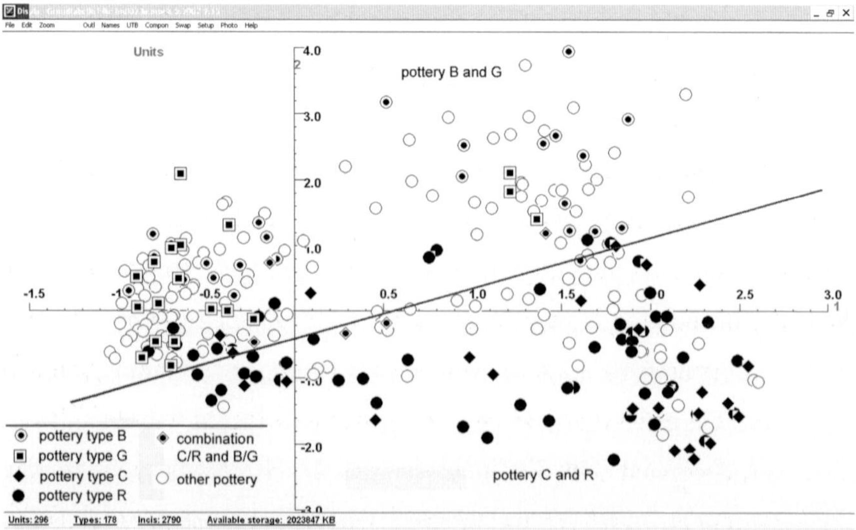

Fig. 57: Correspondence analysis: Distribution of the most distinct pottery types

of the body with amulets. The burial pose was therefore secondary. A second result is the fact that pottery types B and G were found with extended burials, and pottery types C and R with non-extended. Even if we cannot explain the difference, since we are not able to interpret the codes of communication and representation, it is obvious that there are, according to the archaeological material, main groups and subgroups. These can be clearly defined and have only small areas of overlapping.

Grave 1516

As we have already seen even though there are more or less homogenous groups, there are still a few single burials which differ significantly. I assume that these burials communicate specific identities, which were understood in the given society as well. One particular grave in the whole cemetery is really striking. This remarkable burial combines several objects which are exceptional in the cemetery of Sanam. We have no way of explaining the status or function of this person, but here is a possibility to appreciate an individual identity.

The burial itself was quite normal: an extended body in a bricked tomb. But the adornment is unique in this cemetery and some objects even unique for the Napatan period as a whole. The head was covered by a cap or veil with udjat eyes, the forehead with a golden strip. On the upper body and upper arms discs of bronze were found – were these appliqués on a coat? On the breast were seven big faience plaques with loop holes. They are decorated with kneeling figures of Heh or Nile gods (colour plate 24). On an eighth plaque, are representations of a standing figure of Onuris and a lion-headed goddess (colour plate 25). These plaques as well as the bronze discs are the only examples from the cemetery.

The jewellery on the arms is very exceptional. On both lower arms the deceased had bronze cuffs which covered four armlets. These cuffs are known from the costume of the Meroitic ruler, but they are unique in Napatan times. On the upper arm the deceased wore a faience armlet with a single open-worked decoration (see fig. 36). There were also ivory armlets.

Besides all these special and otherwise unknown objects the deceased was decorated with quantities of amulets, beads, scarabs and rings (four together on one finger of the left hand!).

All in all, in grave 1516 we are confronted with a unique burial in this cemetery and since the dimensions and the style of the tomb itself is quite normal, we should think on the individual's personal influence in the choice of the objects.

III.5.3. Summary

In the rich material of the cemetery of Sanam we can identify specific groups and investigate them one by one. By doing this, we can distinguish subgroups which have no clear boundaries, but small overlapping areas. The correspondence analysis arranges burials according to their similarity and visualise this order in the depiction of points in space. This provides us with the possibility to summarise subgroups. The unifying and separate elements which are expressed by the "factors" in the correspondence analysis have to be interpreted archaeologically.

With the distinguishing elements, the groups express the "we" – the collective group identity. There are the norms of representation of every group which makes them distinctive. Within these groups there is another level with a code system representing the various subgroups. And again within these subgroups, there are some single burials which use their individual freedom within the habitus of the society to represent their own identity.

IV. Fragments of the Napatan society

In the forgoing chapters, we discussed the (available) material from the cemetery of Sanam in different views. Chronological as well as geographical aspects, hierarchical and the cultural framework were explored. Finally, we reached the individual and his freedom to represent himself within the borders of the habitus of the society. In this final chapter we will bring together the various aspects to present a picture of the funerary society at Sanam. Of course, this picture will remain fragmentary, since we lack important sources which were destroyed or not documented by Griffith. Moreover, I could only investigate a few objects intensively, all the others I know only from the description and photographs of Griffith.

IV.1. The structure of the funerary society at Sanam (fig. 58)

In the chapter on individual characteristics apparent in the cemetery it was already stated that there were several more or less homogeneous classes of burials which can be distinguished clearly from others. Although some elements overlap, we can deduce for example a cluster of burials determined by "bead net and/or cartonnage". Now, we can try to find more (or all) classes hidden in the material culture of the cemetery at Sanam. Again, we will use the correspondence analysis to locate all burials in the multi-dimensional space. Clusters of the representations as scatter plots can be summarised as classes of burials. And again we will use the theory of P. Bourdieu, who understood the agents of a society as represented in the cultural space.[113] But contrary to Bourdieu, we do not know which factors constitute the axis of this space. For him, it was

[113] Bourdieu 1985.

economic, social, cultural and symbolic wealth. We have to deduce the factors from their representation as scatter plots.

In this short summary of the whole investigation of the cemetery at Sanam, I cannot explain all the correspondence analyses and all the stages of interpretation I made. I made separate analyses using all graves, all burials, burials with objects and intact burials, and examined up to four axes. With these, I was able to define the following co-ordinates for the field "burial in Sanam". Because of the problematic situation with the sources it was necessary for me to construct the system on two levels – graves respectively burials – in order that they did not merge completely.

IV.1.1. Graves (fig. 59)

The x-axis or first and most prominent factor seems to be the energy invested by the people in order to build the grave (fig. 60). Cave graves are situated at one end of the graphic, sand burials at the other end. Next to the cave graves are stairway tombs and then lateral niche graves. Of course, there can be a chronological aspect hidden behind this distribution, but we cannot be sure about that. Visible for us through the correspondence analysis is the range from simple to elaborate graves.

The second factor (y-axis) is constituted by the appearance of finds. Here, the dots representing cave graves and sand burials are near to each other, since very often both of them lack finds. Again, there is the problem of what process lay behind this distribution pattern: it could represent the richness (or lack thereof) of the burial or the stage after its robbery.

The categories of finds form the third factor (z-axis): at one end are the amulets, situated at the other end is the pottery. The idea behind these categories could relate to the provisioning for the afterlife: magical – with amulets – or material, with real goods – pottery and its contents.

All the graves at Sanam can now be plotted in order to construct these three dimensions: according to the energy expended in building the grave, according to the amount of objects, and according to the category of provisioning for the afterlife. These dots can be summarised into clusters which form theoretical groups. If these archaeological clusters can be connected with real "social" clusters, we will never know.

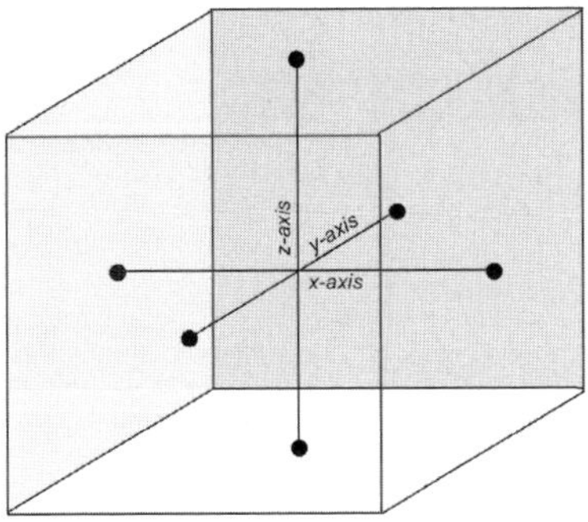

Fig. 58: Three-dimensional pattern of the two-dimensional view of the construction of the social fields with the representation of the three co-ordinates

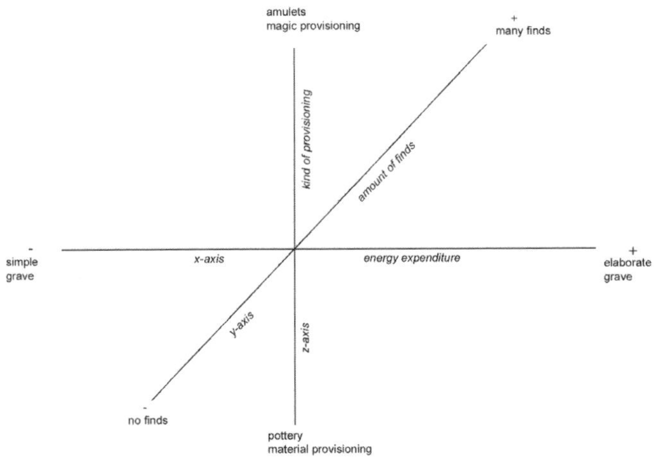

Fig. 59: Construction of the field „burial customs in Sanam" – layer of the graves

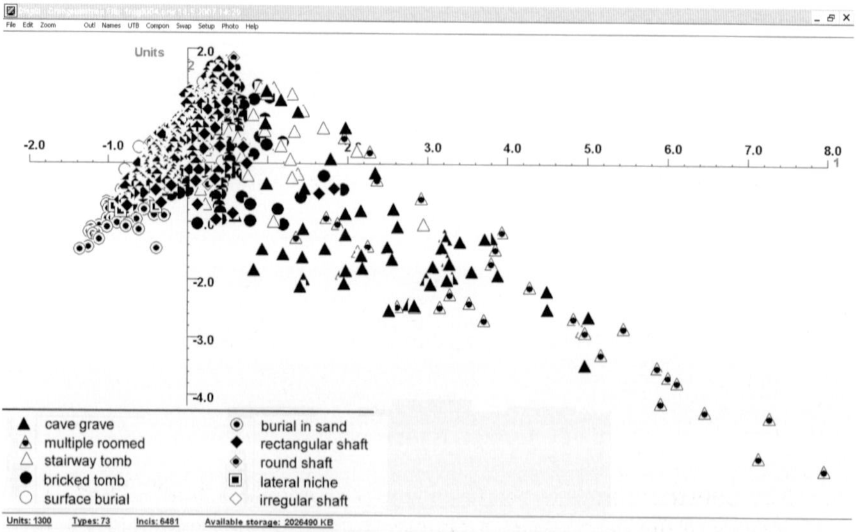

Fig. 60: Correspondence analysis: All graves with marked grave types

IV.1.2. Burials (fig. 61)

In the second level we investigate the burials in the same manner. Since we lack burials and finds especially in the cave and stairway graves, most of the graves with high energy expenditure are excluded.

Therefore, the x-axis of the level of the graves is not structured at the level of the burials. The main factor at the level of the burials is the equipment with amulets (fig. 62). At one end of the scale are burials with many amulets; at the other end are burials without amulets (but with pottery, bead net and/or cartonnage, or without any finds). I interpret the x-axis as the degree of intensity of magical equipment.

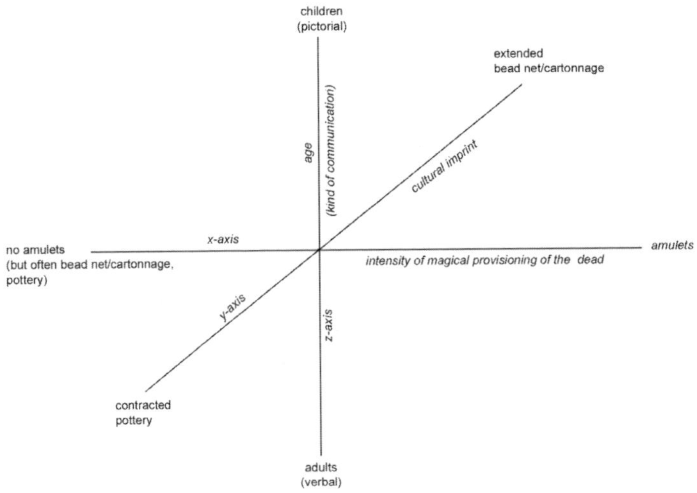

Fig. 61: Construction of the field „burial customs in Sanam"– layer of the burials of the graves with high energy expenditure are excluded.

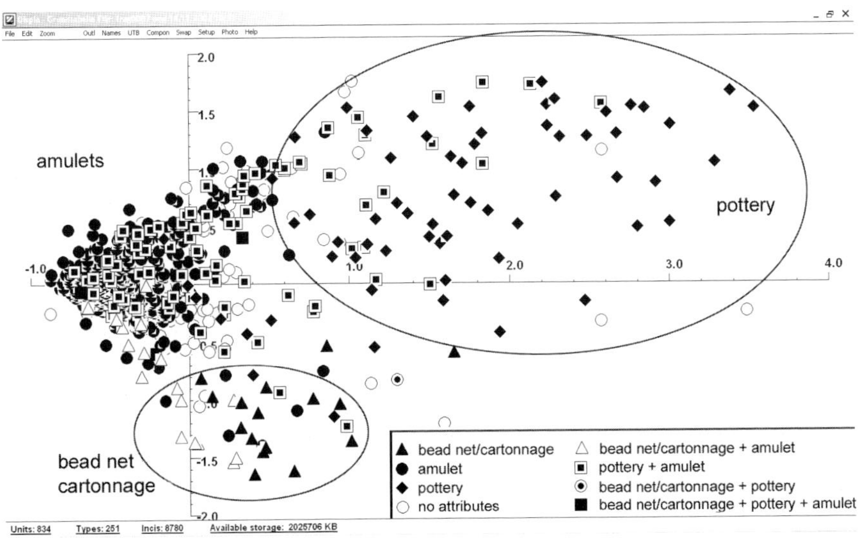

Fig. 62: Correspondence analysis: Burials with objects, with marked categories (detail of the correspondence analysis)

The second factor is constituted by two interconnected elements: the burial pose (extended vs. non-extended, fig. 63) and the equipment with pottery at one end and bead net/cartonnage at the other end. Perhaps a cultural or ideological concept lies behind this distribution, therefore I call it the cultural imprint.

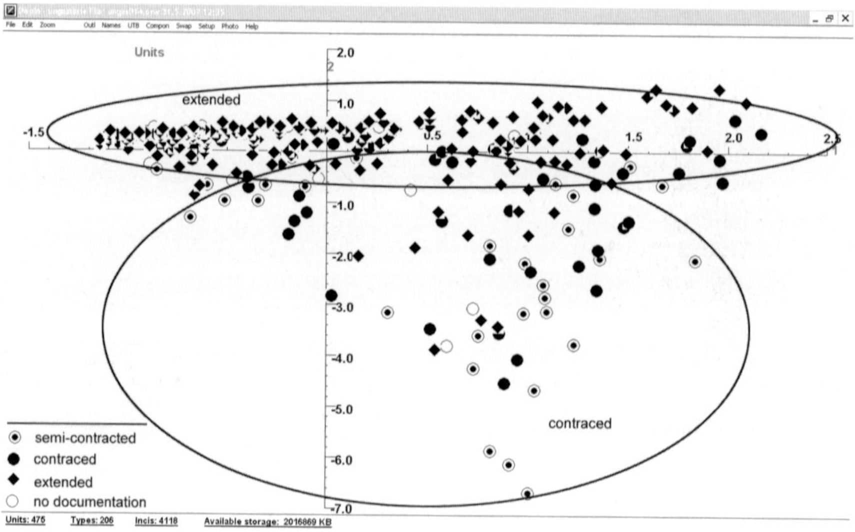

Fig. 63: Correspondence analysis: All intact graves, marked burial poses

The z-axis is determined by the age of the buried persons (fig. 64). At one end are figural amulets (mainly found with children) and at the other end inscribed scarabs (mainly found with adults). We can explain it as pictorial vs. verbal magical equipment.

Again, we can distribute the burials using dots in the technical space and summarise them as clusters. But of course there are many problems with the interpretation of the concepts behind the (technical) axis: for the y-axis we can state that the cultural imprint seems to be relevant, but why the specific combination of elements was chosen for every burial remains unknown. We have to bear in mind that these are analytical groups, established on the basis of fragmentary sources.

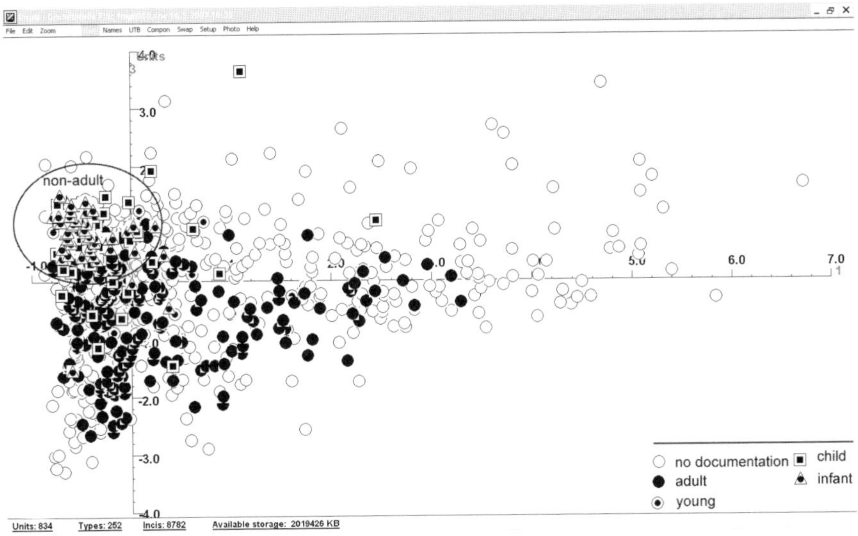

Fig. 64: Correspondence analysis: Burials, marked age, 1st and 3rd components

It is not possible to connect both levels – the graves and the burials. There are similar formative factors for the construction of the (technical) social space, but these are on different axes. Therefore we can only summarise the various aspects: For the graves the "investment" is the most structuring factor, on the level of the burials it is the intensity of magical provisioning. The cultural imprint is relevant for both levels. On the level charting burials, the age of the dead is an important factor, which is expressed by the symbolic communication system.

IV.1.3. The funerary community at Sanam

In the cemetery of Sanam we can trace the funerary community of a privileged town. The town's geographical position at the main crossroads of the empire and its proximity to the royal cemeteries facilitated access to luxury goods. The cemetery is formed with various different combinations of specific elements. This method is not unusual in other Napatan cemeteries. Prominent in this cemetery is the contemporary construction of burials with contrasting cultural patterns. We can identify the core groups of "extended + bead net/cartonnage", "extended + amulets", and "non-extended + pottery". These groups were already noted by Griffith, but now we can observe that they overlap each other and that there was flexibility in the choice of the elements. There exist several context-dependent, maybe competing, classifications which represent themselves as hybrid identities in the archaeological context.

Since we cannot establish a detailed chronology for the main phase in the first half of the Napatan period, it is possible to interpret the overlapping patterns of the groups with chronological influence. In this interpretation, the clear boundaries of the different groups were blurred with the passage of time. However, if the boundaries are not defined by chronological changes, we have to accept that the presentation of identities and the hold on traditions was more likely to have been influenced by the actors than we generally assume for antique societies.

IV.2. Funerary praxis in the cemetery of Sanam

Up to now we have focused on elements, patterns and structures. The inhabitants of Sanam lived in a system which determined them within the boundaries of the habitus, but which they formed by themselves through their actions. We have located the burials in the (technical) space of the x-, y- and z-co-ordinates and are therefore presented in their position relative to one another. Some burials are situated very near to each other but none are really the same, as each one is distinguished by its own subtle distinctions.[114] Every burial is individual, even if collectively most of the burials look much the same. The differences are subtle, but they are visible in the archaeological record. Therefore, besides the overall structure of the funerary culture represented at Sanam, we can also grasp distinct individual decisions.

In this last chapter I want to focus on the actions taken for the burial. First of all, since there are Napatan graves, we can assume that the practice to bury the dead was fixed in the mentality of these people. But like in Egypt and other regions in Nubia, we lack many tombs and their occupants. Even if both sexes, all ages and all social classes are represented at Sanam, there are still too few children documented for an average ancient funerary society. We will never know if there was an internal decision regarding which children were to be buried there or if the lack of evidence is caused by erosion or destruction.

The burial itself is one of the *rites de passage*, when the person was excluded from the society of the living and included in the society of the dead.[115] Even though we cannot explain the changes in the society at Sanam, we can point out some traces relating to the burial. When the dead left the community of the living, they were isolated in space. The graves are situated in the cemetery and are separated from the town. There, the dead were buried – the separation is not only horizontal, but also a vertical distance. Most of the graves were built before the burial took place: the shafts were dug, the bricked tombs built, the family graves, like cave

---

[114] Bourdieu 1984

[115] For an overview on “burials” see Parker-Pearson 1999.

graves, reopened. Only the sand graves may have been prepared at the same time as the burial. It is likely that several people were involved in the funeral. The deceased was transported to the cemetery, the grave was built. It is likely that there were bereaved – whether they were family and friends or professional mourners remains unclear.

The dead was interred, sometimes earlier burials were put aside. At this time the grave goods were also put into the grave. After the closing of the tomb, burials rites were made at the entrance or above the tomb. Griffith documented offering tables and incense burners especially with cave graves; perhaps the small amount of pottery found outside some graves is connected with these burial rites too. The lack of evidence for rituals at most of the graves should not be taken as proof that these rituals did not take place. It is possible that this activity has left no visible trace in archaeology .

The appearance of the deceased in the burial seems to be an important factor. Most of them were interred with adornments, some very simple, others more elaborate. Together with various kinds of jewellery, amulets were also attached to the corpse. This hints to the magical protection of the dead.

In a few cases, the deceased was covered with a bead net and/or cartonnage. We can assume that under the bead net the corpse was veiled with a cloth, but no evidence for this has remained.

Apart from the dead, the grave goods, too, were a form of presentation. The burial is the moment when the presentation of status, wealth and identity was possible. However, we cannot interpret differences in gender or specific roles, since we have no written evidence from this cemetery.

With the documented archaeological remains from Sanam, we can at least partly reconstruct the funerary practices of the Napatan inhabitants.

IV.3. Summary

This investigation seeks to individualise the funerary community of the cemetery at Sanam. It is a complex society with a variety of traditions and specific practices. Firstly, I have attempted to put in order all the information left by Griffith in order to define the structure of the cemetery. The framework was developed using chronological, topographical, hierarchical, cultural and individual aspects. And from the mass of 1619 graves and 1560 burials we reached the individual. Finally, I have gone further and attempted to construct the Napatan society at Sanam. The result reflects the conceptual frame of action each person had. The wide range of choices and the combinations of elements present in the cemetery hints at the complex alternatives available to the population within this habitual frame. There are significant core groups visible in the archaeological context, but the potential of identifying individuality is visible as well.

LITERATURE

Cited literature

Adams, W.Y. (1977), Nubia. Corridor to Africa, Princeton, Londres

Addison, F. (1949), Jebel Moya. The Wellcome Excavations in the Sudan, Oxford

Aston, D.A. (2009), Burial Assemblages of Dynasty 21-25. Chronology – Typology – Developments, Vienna

Berenguer F. (2004), Excavations at the New Royal Cemetery at Gebel Barkal (Karima, Sudan), in: Kendall, T. (ed.), Nubian Studies 1998. Proceedings of the Ninth Conference of the International Society of Nubian Studies, Boston: 223-227

Berger-El Naggar, C./ Leclant, J. (2006-2007), Contribution à l'étude du Méroitique final entre IIe et IIIe Cataracte, in: Gratien, B. (ed.), Mélanges offerts à Francis Geus, CRIPEL 26: 41-45

Bonnet, C. (1999), The funerary traditions of Middle Nubia, in: Welsby, D. (ed.), Recent Research in Kushite History and Archaeology. Proceedings of the 8th International Conference for Meroitic Studies, London: 1-9

Bourdieu, P. (1977), Outline of a Theory of Practice, Cambridge

Bourdieu, P. (1984), Distinction: A Social Critique of the Judgement of Taste, Boston

Bourdieu, P. (1985), Sozialer Raum und „Klassen". Leçon sur la leçon. Zwei Vorlesungen. Frankfurt/M.

Budka, J. (2007), Documentation and excavation of dome and crevice graves in Kirbekan, in: C. Näser, M. Lange (ed.), The Archaeology and Ethnography of the Fourth Nile Cataract. Proceedings of the Second International Conference on the Archaeology of the Fourth Nile Cataract, Berlin, 4-6 August 2005, Meroitica 23: 73-90

Bultè, J. (2008), "Cuillers d'offrandes" en faience et en pierre messagères de bien-être et de prospérité, RdE 59: 1-17

Dunham, D. (1950), El Kurru. The Royal Cemeteries of Kush I, Published for The Museum of Fine Arts, Cambridge, Mass.

Dunham, D. (1955), Nuri. The Royal Cemeteries of Kush II, Boston

Dunham, D. (1963), The West and South Cemeteries at Meroe. The Royal Cemeteries of Kush V, Boston

Eisa, K.A. (1999), Le mobilier et les coutumes funéraires koushites à l'époque méroitique, Meroitica 16, Berlin

FHN I, T. Eide/T. Hägg/R.H. Pierce/L. Török (Hrsg.), Fontes Historiae Nubiorum. Textual Sources for the History of the Middle Nile Region between the Eigth Cent. BC and the Sixth Cent. AD. Vol. I: From the Eigth to the Mid-Fifth Cent. BC, Bergen 1994

French, P. (1986), Late Dynastic Pottery from the Vicinity of the South Tombs, in: Kemp, B., Amarna Reports III, London: 147-188

Gerharz, R. (1994), Jebel Moya, Meroitica 14, Berlin

Geus, F. (1975), Le cimetière de la XXVe dynastie (MF-NE), in: Vercoutter, J., Mirgissa II. Les nécropoles, Paris: 479-501

Geus, F. (1984), Rescuing Sudan Ancient Cultures, Khartoum

Geus, F./ Lecointe, Y./ Maureille, B. (1995), Tombes napateennes, méroitiques et médievales de la necropole nord de l'île de Sai. Rapport preliminaire de la campagne 1994-1995 (Archéologie et anthropologie), ANM 7: 99-141

Gotter, U. (2001), "Akkulturation" als Methodenproblem der historischen Wissenschaften, in: Altekamp S./ Hofter, M./ Krumme, M. (Hg.), Posthumanistische Klassische Archäologie. Historizität und Wissenschaftlichkeit von Interessen und Methoden, München: 255-280

Griffith, F.Ll. (1922), Oxford Excavations in Nubia. VIII-XVII, Napata, Sanam Temple, Treasury and Town, LAAA 9: 67-124

Griffith, F.Ll. (1923), Oxford Excavations in Nubia. XVIII-XXV, The Cemetery of Sanam, LAAA 10: 73-171

Hintze, F. (1979), Elemente der meroitischen Kultur, Meroitica 5: 101-105

Hogarth, D.G. (1922), Engraved Hittite Objects, JEA 8: 211-218

Jaeger, B. (1982), Essai de classification et datation des scarabées Menkhéperrê, OBO-SerArch 2

Janot, F./ Berger, C./ Cartier, F./ Martin, J./ Labrousse, A. (1997), Observations sur la phase d'activité napatéenne de la nécropole de Sedeinga, CRIPEL 17/2: 129-135

Kendall, T. (1982), Kush: Lost Kingdom of the Nile, Brockton

Kormysheva, E. (2006), Gods and Divine Symbols of the Ancient Sudanese Civilisation: Catalogue of the Sudan National Museum in Khartoum, Moskow

LD, Lepsius, C.R., Denkmaeler aus Aegypten und Aethiopien, 12 Bände und Ergänzungsband, Berlin (1849-1859)

LDT, Lepsius, C.R., Denkmaeler aus Aegypten und Aethiopien, Text (Hrsg. E. Naville), 5 Bände, Leipzig (1897–1913)

Lohwasser, A. (2002a), Eine phönizische Bronzeschale aus dem Sudan, Ä&L 12: 221-234

Lohwasser, A. (2002b), Gefahren lauern überall. Zu den Tiermotiven auf einem Amulett aus Sanam, Der antike Sudan, MittSAG 13: 47-58

Lohwasser, A. (2006a), News from Sanam, in: 11th International Conference of Nubian Studies, Warsaw University, 27 August - 2 September 2006, Abstracts: 38-39

Lohwasser, A. (2006b), Ein archäologischer Beleg für einen kuschitischen Kopfschmuck, Der antike Sudan, MittSAG 17: 121-125

Lohwasser, A. (2007), Ein Nordländer im Südland. Zu einem ägyptischen Spendenlöffel aus dem Sudan, Der antike Sudan, MittSAG 18: 179-188

Lohwasser, A. (2010), News from the cemetery of Sanam, in: W. Godlewski, A. Łajtar (eds), Between the Cataracts, Proceedings of the 11th International Conference for Nubian Studies, Warsaw University, 27 August - 2 September 2006, Part Two: Session Papers [=PAM Supplement Series, vol. 2.1-2], Warsaw 2010: 455-459

Lohwasser, A. (forthcoming), A Kushite bronze implement and its modern African descendants, in: M. Zach (ed.), The Kushite World. Proceedings of the 11th International Conference for Meroitic Studies, Vienna, 1-4

September 2008
Macadam, M.F.L. (1949), The Temples of Kawa I. The Inscriptions, London
Morkot, R. (2000), The Black Pharaohs. Egypt's Nubian Rulers, London
Mukherjee, R./ Rao, C.R./ Trevor, J.C. (1955), The Ancient Inhabitants of Jebel Moya (Sudan). Occasional Publications of the Cambridge University Museum of Archaeology and Ethnology 3
Näser C. (2006), Die Humboldt University Nubian Expedition 2006. Arbeiten auf Us und Mograt, Der antike Sudan. MittSAG 17: 89-116
Parker-Pearson, M. (1999), The archaeology of death and burial, London
PM, Porter, B./R. Moss, Topographical Bibliography of Ancient Egyptian Hieroglyphic Texts, Reliefs, and Paintings, Vol. I–VII, Oxford
Pohl, W. (1998), Introduction: Strategies of distinction, in: Pohl, W./ Reimitz, H. (Hg.), Strategies of distinction: the construction of the ethnic communities, 300-800, Leiden: 1-15
Säve-Söderbergh, T. e.a. (1989), Middle Nubian Sites (SJE 4), Stockholm
Schäfer, H. (1895), Die äthiopische Königsinschrift des Louvre, ZÄS 33: 101-113
Schiff-Giorgini, M. (1966), Sedeinga, 1964-1965, Kush 14: 244-261
Seiler, A. (2005), Tradition & Wandel. Die Keramik als Spiegel der Kulturentwicklung Thebens in der Zweiten Zwischenzeit, SDAIK 32
Silvano, F. (1980), Le reticelle funerarie nell'antico Egitto: Proposte di Interpretazione, EVO 3: 83–97
Smith, St.T. (1992), Intact Tombs of the Seventeenth and Eighteenth Dynasties from Thebes and the New Kingdom Burial System, MDAIK 48: 193-231
Smith, S.T. (2003), Wretched Kush. Ethnic Identities and Boundaries in Egypt's Nubian Empire, London/New York
Smith, S.T. (2006-2007), A new Napatan Cemetery at Tombos, in: Gratien, B. (ed.), Mélanges offerts à Francis Geus, CRIPEL 26: 347-352
Spencer, P. (2002), Amara West. II. The cemetery and the pottery corpus, London
Taylor, B. (1893), Journey to Central Africa; or, Life and Landscapes from Eypt to the Negro Kingdoms of the White Nile, New York/ London
Vila, A. (1980a), La prospection archéologique de la Vallée du Nil, au sud de la cataracte de Dal (Nubie Soudanaise). Fasc. 12: La nécropole de Missiminia. I. Les sépultures napatéennes, Paris
Vila, A., (1980b), Les tombes napateennes "sans mobilier", *MNL* 20: 29-41
Vincentelli, I. (2004), Excavation at Sanam Abu Dom, Abstracts of the 10th International Conference for Meroitic Studies, Paris, Sept.1 – Sept. 4 2004: 21
Vincentelli, I. (2006), Hillat el-Arab. The Joint Sudanese-Italian Expedition in the Napatan Region, Sudan, BAR International Series 1570, Oxford
Vincentelli, I. (2006-2007), Some Clay Sealings from Sanam Abu Dom, in: Gratien, B. (ed.), Mélanges offerts à Francis Geus, CRIPEL 26: 371-378
Vincentelli, I. (2007), Ritorno a Sanam, Pharaon Magazine 2007/2: 8-17
Welsby D.A. (2001), Life on the Desert Edge. Seven thousand years of settlement in the Northern Dongola Reach, Sudan. BAR 980, Oxford
Welsby D.A. (2002), The Kushite Town and Cemetery at Kawa. Survey and Excavations, Sudan & Nubia 6: 32-37

Welsby, D. (2004), The SARS Amri to Kirbekan Survey: Excavations at the pyramid, Site 4-F-71, Sudan & Nubia 8: 2-3
Williams, B.B. (1990), The University of Chicago Oriental Institute Nubian Expedition. Vol. VII: Twenty-Fifth Dynasty and Napatan Remains at Qustul: Cemeteries W and V, Chicago
Williams, B.B. (1993), The University of Chicago Oriental Institute Nubian Expedition. Vol. X: Excavations at Serra East, A-Group, C-Group, Pan Grave, New Kingdom, and X-Group Remains from Cemeteries A-G and Rock Shelters, Chicago
Zibelius-Chen, K. (2006), The Chronology of Nubian Kingdoms from Dyn. 25 to the End of the Kingdom of Meroe, in: Hornung, E./ Krauss, R./ Warburton, D.A. (ed.), Ancient Egyptian Chronology, HdO I.38: 284-303
Zurawski, B. (1998), Archaeological Reconnaissance in the Abkor/Tergis Area, GAMAR 1: 133-143
Zurawski, B. (2005), The Temple of Soniyat, 1998-2002, GAMAR 3: 289-302

Further reading

Adams, W.Y. (1977), Nubia. Corridor to Africa, Princeton, Londres
Bonnet, C. (1999), The funerary traditions of Middle Nubia, in: Welsby, D. (ed.), Recent Research in Kushite History and Archaeology. Proceedings of the 8th International Conference for Meroitic Studies, London: 1-9
Brather, S. (2004), Ethnische Interpretationen in der frühgeschichtlichen Archäologie. Geschichte, Grundlagen, Alternativen; Ergänzungsbände zum Reallexikon der Germanischen Altertumskunde 42, Berlin/New York
Edwards, D.N. (1996), The Archaeology of the Meroitic State. New perspectives on its social and political organisation, BAR International Series 640, Oxford
Edwards, D.N. (2004), The Nubian Past. An Archaeology of the Sudan, London/New York
Fitzenreiter, M. (2004), Identität als Bekenntnis und Anspruch – Notizen zum Grab des Pennut (Teil IV), in: Der antike Sudan. MittSAG 15: 169-193
Grajetzki, W. (2003), Burial Customs in Ancient Egypt. Life in Death for Rich and Poor, London
Jones, S. (1997), The Archaeology of Ethnicity: Constructing Identities in the Past and the Present, London/New York
Kendall, T. (1999), The Origin of the Napatan State: El-Kurru and the Evidence for the Royal Ancestors, Meroitica 15: 3-117
Lohwasser, A. (2001), Die königlichen Frauen im antiken Reich von Kusch. 25. Dynastie bis zur Zeit des Nastasen, Meroitica 19
Priese, K.-H. (1996), Das Reich von Napata und Meroe, in: Wildung, D. (Hg.), Sudan. Antike Königreiche am Nil, München: 207-217

Seidlmayer, St.J. (1988), Funerärer Aufwand und soziale Ungleichheit. Eine methodische Anmerkung zum Problem der Rekonstruktion der gesellschaftlichen Gliederung aus Friedhofsfunden, GM 104: 25-51

Seidlmayer, St. J. (2002): Nubier im ägyptischen Kontext im Alten und Mittleren Reich, Mitteilungen des SFB „Differenz und Integration“ 2: Akkulturation und Selbstbehauptung, Orientwissenschaftliche Hefte 4/2002, Halle/Wittenberg: 89–113.

Török, L. (1997), The Kingdom of Kush: Handbook of Napatan-Meroitic Civilisation. HdO 1. 31, Leiden

Veit, U./ Kienlin, T.L./ Kümmel, C./ Schmidt, S. (2003), Spuren und Botschaften: Interpretationen materieller Kultur, TÄT 4

Welsby D.A. (1996), The Kingdom of Kush. The Napatan and Meroitic empires, London